Apress Pocket Guides

Apress Pocket Guides present concise summaries of cutting-edge developments and working practices throughout the tech industry. Shorter in length, books in this series aims to deliver quick-to-read guides that are easy to absorb, perfect for the time-poor professional.

This series covers the full spectrum of topics relevant to the modern industry, from security, AI, machine learning, cloud computing, web development, product design, to programming techniques and business topics too.

Typical topics might include:

- A concise guide to a particular topic, method, function or framework

- Professional best practices and industry trends

- A snapshot of a hot or emerging topic

- Industry case studies

- Concise presentations of core concepts suited for students and those interested in entering the tech industry

- Short reference guides outlining 'need-to-know' concepts and practices.

More information about this series at https://link.springer.com/bookseries/17385.

Quantum Security

Revolutionizing Network Security with Digital IDs

Christopher Murphy

Apress®

Quantum Security: Revolutionizing Network Security with Digital IDs

Christopher Murphy
Clearwater, FL, USA

ISBN-13 (pbk): 979-8-8688-1239-2   ISBN-13 (electronic): 979-8-8688-1240-8
https://doi.org/10.1007/979-8-8688-1240-8

Managing Director, Apress Media LLC: Welmoed Spahr
Acquisitions Editor: Susan McDermott
Development Editor: Laura Berendson
Project Manager: Jessica Vakili

Cover designed by eStudioCalamar

Distributed to the book trade worldwide by Springer Science+Business Media New York, 1 New York Plaza, New York, NY 10004. Phone 1-800-SPRINGER, fax (201) 348-4505, e-mail orders-ny@springer-sbm.com, or visit www.springeronline.com. Apress Media, LLC is a California LLC and the sole member (owner) is Springer Science + Business Media Finance Inc (SSBM Finance Inc). SSBM Finance Inc is a **Delaware** corporation.

For information on translations, please e-mail booktranslations@springernature.com; for reprint, paperback, or audio rights, please e-mail bookpermissions@springernature.com.

Apress titles may be purchased in bulk for academic, corporate, or promotional use. eBook versions and licenses are also available for most titles. For more information, reference our Print and eBook Bulk Sales web page at http://www.apress.com/bulk-sales.

If disposing of this product, please recycle the paper

To my wife AnnMarie, whose unwavering support has made it possible for my thoughts to find their way to paper. For over 30 years, she has been my guide, researching, reading technical documents, and helping me stay informed despite my dyslexia. Her gift for uncovering key insights has been invaluable.

To my children, who have sacrificed so much for my work. Your belief in science and constant encouragement through the hardest times mean more than words can express. I am endlessly grateful for your faith and support.

Table of Contents

About the Author

Christopher Murphy is a cybersecurity expert and pioneer in digital identity and secure network interaction. With over 25 years of experience in the field, Chris has worked with private organizations and government agencies, developing innovative solutions to eliminate vulnerabilities in network security. He is the inventor of Existence Authentication Identification (EAID) technology, a groundbreaking approach to direct user interaction, and has dedicated his career to addressing cybersecurity's most persistent challenges. This book is his effort to share these insights with a broader audience and offer actionable solutions to a broken system.

Preface

Network security has become a paramount concern for businesses, governments, and individuals alike. The past few decades have witnessed an unprecedented rise in cyber threats, from phishing schemes and ransomware attacks to sophisticated identity theft and corporate espionage. The Internet, once seen as a limitless frontier of opportunity, has increasingly become a battlefield where sensitive information and critical infrastructure are under constant siege.

Yet, despite the growing complexity of these threats, much of the cybersecurity industry has remained anchored in outdated methods and misconceptions. The traditional approach to cybersecurity, rooted in convenience and quick fixes, has led to a system that is often more reactive than proactive, more focused on damage control than on true prevention. As a result, we find ourselves in a world where breaches are not only common but expected, where the very tools designed to protect us are frequently compromised.

This book challenges the status quo. It argues that the real issue in cybersecurity is not just about technology; it's about the choices we've made, choices that have prioritized ease of use over true security, that have allowed critical vulnerabilities to persist, and that have ultimately placed networks at risk. The central premise of this book is that these choices, and the underlying assumptions that drive them, must be reexamined if we are to achieve the level of security that the digital age demands.

At the heart of this reexamination is the concept of direct user interaction through digital identifications (IDs). This approach, which diverges from the indirect, browser-based and installed software–based methods that have dominated cybersecurity, offers a fundamentally new way to secure networks. It emphasizes the importance of proving not just identity but presence and of doing so in a manner that aligns with the principles of true multifactor authentication (MFA).

The chapters that follow will guide you through this new paradigm, exploring the science of authentication, the flaws in current cybersecurity practices, and the transformative potential of digital IDs. You will discover how these innovations can eliminate many of the common security issues that plague networks today and why the adoption of such methods is not just a technological upgrade but a necessary evolution.

This book is written for those who recognize that the stakes in cybersecurity are higher than ever. It is for business leaders, security professionals, and anyone who understands that the cost of inaction is far greater than the investment in real, lasting solutions. As you read, I encourage you to think critically about the systems you rely on and to consider the profound impact that a shift in approach could have, not just for your organization but for the broader digital ecosystem.

In a world where cyber threats are constant and evolving, it's time to stop playing defense and start taking control. The path to true network security begins here, with a commitment to integrity, innovation, and the courage to embrace change.

Introduction

In the constantly evolving world of cybersecurity, where threats grow more sophisticated and breaches become more common, defending against these challenges can often seem overwhelming. For decades, the industry has responded by layering one mitigation strategy on top of another, creating a patchwork of defenses that, while effective in the short term, often feels more like a temporary fix than a permanent solution. This approach, rooted in complexity, has led to a labyrinth in the security environment where the focus is on treating symptoms rather than addressing the underlying causes of vulnerabilities.

At the heart of this approach lies a critical flaw, a binary mistake that has shaped the entire cybersecurity industry: the reliance on public access models and the assumption that identity can be verified through complex, transmitted data. This foundational error has not only compromised the security of networks but has also perpetuated a cycle of breach and mitigation that is endless. Each new layer of security, while adding a level of protection, also introduces new points of failure, creating an increasingly fragile system.

The purpose of this book is to confront that mistake head-on and to present a clear, unequivocal alternative that can finally break this cycle. The technology behind digital IDs and direct user interaction offers a powerful solution, but it is not a silver bullet for all cybersecurity challenges. Instead, it addresses a specific and fundamental issue, the first and most critical mistake in the stack, by moving the verification of user identity entirely off the public Internet. This is not just a technological shift; it's a security revolution, grounded in the binary principles of computer science that have been overlooked and neglected for too long.

At the core of this revolution is a simple yet profound question: How does an authorized user on a secure network prove their identity? The answer is binary; it is either through a digital identification (digital ID) or through the transmission of complex data. Every major exploit that has plagued network security, from public access breaches to identity theft, can be traced back to the decision to allow public logins that rely on data transmission for authentication. This is an irrefutable fact, one that underpins the entire security infrastructure we rely on today.

However, although digital IDs provide a robust solution to this particular problem, they are not a cure-all for every security issue. The presence or absence of a specific individual on a network is just one piece of the puzzle. Yet, when applied judiciously, digital IDs offer a new and powerful tool in the cybersecurity arsenal: a tool that verifies a user's existence in a way that no other technology can. This shift from guessing identity to proving existence changes the dynamic of security, offering a proactive rather than reactive approach.

This book is not just a critique of past mistakes; it is a call to action for the future. It challenges the status quo, urging businesses, governments, and security professionals to rethink their approach to network security. The time has come to move beyond the endless cycle of mitigation and to embrace a new paradigm, one that is rooted in the binary truth of security. The transition to this new model requires a willingness to challenge entrenched beliefs and to recognize that complexity does not necessarily equate to security. Simplicity, grounded in binary logic, offers a clearer and more robust path forward.

As you journey through these chapters, you will see how this shift from cybersecurity to true network security is not just possible but essential. The science and technology are ready; the only question is whether we have the will to take the first step. The stakes are high, but so are the rewards: a future where networks are not just defended but inherently secure, where trust is not assumed but proven, and where the integrity of our digital lives is preserved.

Based on an estimated reading time of approximately 3 minutes (calculated at 200 words per minute for 648 words), the potential damage cost if compromised is estimated at $57 million. This calculation underscores the critical importance of implementing integrity-based security measures to prevent unauthorized access and mitigate associated risks.

CHAPTER 1

The Origins of Cybersecurity

Cybersecurity, as we know it today, is a field born out of necessity. In a world where digital information has become the lifeblood of modern society, the need to protect this information has grown exponentially. But to understand where we are today, we must first look back at the origins of cybersecurity, how it came to be, the decisions that shaped its evolution, and the foundational mistakes that have led to the challenges we face now.

The Birth of the Internet and Initial Vulnerabilities

The story of cybersecurity begins with the birth of the Internet. Originally designed as a network for sharing information among trusted parties, the Internet was built on the principles of openness and accessibility. It was envisioned as a tool for collaboration, an academic and research platform meant to foster the exchange of ideas and knowledge, rather than a battlefield for malicious attacks. The early architects of the Internet were more concerned with making information freely available than with securing it, a mindset that would have far-reaching consequences as the Internet grew beyond its original scope.

© Christopher Murphy 2025
C. Murphy, *Quantum Security*, Apress Pocket Guides,
https://doi.org/10.1007/979-8-8688-1240-8_1

In the 1970s and 1980s, as the Internet began to take shape, the concept of security was not a primary concern. Networks were small, often isolated, and access was limited to a few universities, research institutions, and government bodies. The need for security was minimal because the users were known and trusted, operating in an environment where the notion of cyber threats was virtually nonexistent. The focus was on connectivity, enabling communication between a handful of entities rather than guarding against potential threats.

The Expansion of the Internet and Its Implications

This era of trust and openness set the stage for the Internet's rapid expansion, but it also laid the groundwork for vulnerabilities that would later be exploited on a massive scale. The lack of built-in security features in the original Internet architecture meant that as the network grew, so did its exposure to threats. This initial oversight in design would become a foundational flaw as the Internet evolved into a global network, open to anyone with a connection.

The first major shift came in the 1990s when the Internet became widely accessible to the public. This period marked the transition from a niche tool for researchers and academics to a global phenomenon, transforming every aspect of communication, commerce, and daily life. Suddenly, this tool for collaboration and information sharing was open to anyone with a connection, creating a digital Wild West where new rules and norms were yet to be established.

The Emergence of Cyber Threats

The once-small, isolated networks grew into the vast, interconnected web we know today, the World Wide Web (WWW). This expansion brought with it unprecedented opportunities for businesses, governments, and individuals to connect, share, and innovate. However, it also introduced significant challenges. The open nature of the Internet, once its greatest strength, became its most significant vulnerability. The architects of the early Internet had not anticipated a world where billions of unknown users could access the same network. As the Internet grew, so did the potential for abuse.

The influx of users from all corners of the globe, each with varying degrees of knowledge and intent, created an environment ripe for exploitation. Cybercriminals quickly recognized the opportunities presented by this open network, leading to the first wave of cyber threats that would challenge the very fabric of the Internet.

The Reactive Approach to Cybersecurity

As more people connected to the Internet, the first cyber threats began to appear. These early threats were a stark reminder that the Internet, in its current form, was ill-prepared for the challenges of a connected world. Viruses, worms, and other forms of malware started to spread, exploiting the lack of security in a network's design. These early threats were relatively simple, often created by hobbyists or pranksters, but they highlighted a critical weakness in the Internet's architecture: the lack of built-in security.

The response to these early threats was reactive. As new forms of malware emerged, new security measures were developed to counter them. This reactive approach set the tone for the cybersecurity that would follow. Instead of building security into a network from the ground up, solutions were layered on top of the existing infrastructure, like patches on a leaky boat. This method of addressing security after the fact created a cycle of vulnerability and mitigation, where each new threat prompted a corresponding response, but failed to address the underlying issues.

The Growth of Cybersecurity As a Field

The simplicity of these early threats belied the complexity of the problems they would create. As the Internet expanded and the threats became more sophisticated, the reactive approach to security would prove increasingly inadequate, leading to the development of a new field entirely focused on protecting digital assets: cybersecurity.

The term "cybersecurity" began to gain prominence in the late 1990s and early 2000s as the Internet became a vital part of global commerce, communication, and government operations. The rise of e-commerce, online banking, and digital communication made the need for secure networks more pressing than ever. What was once a niche concern for a small group of technologists had become a critical issue for the global economy.

The Challenge of Public-Facing Logins and Early MFA

Companies and governments began investing heavily in cybersecurity, developing new technologies and protocols to protect their digital assets. Firewalls, encryption, antivirus software, and intrusion detection systems (IDS) became standard tools in the cybersecurity arsenal. However, these tools were often designed to address specific threats rather than provide comprehensive security. The focus remained on patching vulnerabilities as they emerged, rather than rethinking the fundamental design of the network.

This era also saw the emergence of the cybersecurity industry as a significant economic force. Companies specializing in security products and services flourished, offering solutions that promised to protect against the ever-growing array of threats. However, the reliance on reactive security measures meant that the industry was often one step behind the attackers, responding to breaches rather than preventing them.

One of the most critical decisions in the early days of cybersecurity was the choice to maintain public-facing logins for accessing secure networks. This decision was made for the sake of convenience and accessibility, allowing users to access their accounts from anywhere with an Internet connection. However, it also opened the door to a host of security vulnerabilities.

Public logins became a prime target for cybercriminals. Phishing attacks, brute-force attacks, and other forms of exploitation focused on gaining access through these public gateways. The reliance on passwords as the primary form of authentication further compounded the problem, as passwords could be stolen, guessed, or otherwise compromised.

This decision to use public-facing logins was a compromise, one that prioritized convenience over security. It was a trade-off that seemed reasonable at the time, given the nascent state of the Internet and the relatively low level of threat awareness. However, as cyber threats evolved, this compromise would reveal itself as a critical vulnerability, one that cybercriminals would exploit with increasing frequency and sophistication.

The Rise and Challenges of MFA

In response to the growing threat of unauthorized access, multifactor authentication (MFA) was introduced in the early 2000s. The idea was simple: instead of relying on just a password (something you know), users would also need to provide another form of identification for verification, such as a token (something you have) or a fingerprint (something you are).

MFA was a step in the right direction, but it was implemented incorrectly. Many systems still relied on weak forms of authentication, such as SMS-based codes, which could be intercepted or spoofed. Moreover, the fundamental issue of public-facing logins remained unaddressed.

It is the public-facing login that makes MFA a partial solution. Public-facing logins gather factors and transmit data. The network can only perform single-factor authentication (SFA). Multiple data sources or "data attributes" have been equated to multiple factors, a clear misunderstanding of the definition of factor. This misinterpretation led to a false sense of security, as organizations believed they were implementing robust authentication methods, when in reality, they were only adding layers of complexity without addressing the core vulnerability.

Digital IDs and a Missed Opportunity

As MFA was being introduced, the concept of digital identification was also being explored. Digital IDs, which could provide a unique, encrypted identifier for each user, offered a more secure alternative to passwords. Unlike traditional authentication methods that relied on transmitted data, digital IDs represented a form of direct user interaction that could verify not just identity but presence.

The adoption of digital IDs was rejected, however, partly due to the perceived inconvenience of implementing such a system and partly because the technology was still in its infancy. The infrastructure required to support digital IDs was not as widespread or as mature as it is today, leading to concerns about cost, complexity, and user acceptance.

Had digital identification been adopted widely from the start, many of the security issues we face today could have been avoided. Digital IDs would have allowed for a more secure, private interaction with secure networks, eliminating the need for public logins and reducing the risk of unauthorized access. By verifying both identity and presence, digital IDs could have provided a level of security that traditional methods could not match.

The origins of cybersecurity are rooted in a series of decisions made during the early days of the Internet, decisions that prioritized convenience and accessibility over security. These choices laid the groundwork for the challenges we face today, from widespread cyberattacks to the ongoing struggle to implement effective authentication methods. As we move forward, it's essential to learn from these early mistakes.

The journey to a more secure future begins by revisiting the decisions of the past and making the necessary changes to build a more secure Internet for the future. Digital identification and direct user interaction offer a path to a more secure future, one that addresses the root causes of cybersecurity vulnerabilities rather than just treating the symptoms. To achieve this, we must be willing to challenge the status quo, to rethink the assumptions that have guided cybersecurity for decades, and to embrace new technologies and approaches that offer true security in an increasingly connected world.

With an estimated reading time of approximately 9 minutes for 1,707 words, the estimated damage cost if compromised is $171 million.

CHAPTER 2

The Devil Is in the Details

On my first day in computer science class, the professor gave us an assignment that seemed deceptively simple: "Write a paper explaining how to make a peanut butter and jelly sandwich." At first glance, this task appeared trivial, almost laughable in its simplicity. After all, everyone knows how to make a peanut butter and jelly sandwich, right? You just spread the ingredients on two slices of bread and put them together, and you're done. But as I soon discovered, this exercise was not about making a sandwich; it was about teaching us the importance of detailed analysis.

The professor's point was clear: in any complex system, whether it's making a sandwich or securing a network, superficial analysis leads to oversights, and oversights lead to mistakes. In the context of network security, the consequences of such mistakes can be catastrophic.

When you break down the process of making a peanut butter and jelly sandwich, you quickly realize that there are many steps involved, steps that might not be immediately obvious without careful thought, for example:

1. **Gathering Materials:** What kind of bread are you using? Is it fresh? Do you need a knife or a spoon? What about a plate? These are all questions that need answers before you even start spreading anything.

© Christopher Murphy 2025
C. Murphy, *Quantum Security*, Apress Pocket Guides,
https://doi.org/10.1007/979-8-8688-1240-8_2

2. **Ingredient Preparation:** How do you open the jar of peanut butter? Do you need to stir it first if it's a natural peanut butter? What about the jelly? Is it in a squeezable bottle, or do you need to scoop it out with a spoon?

3. **Spreading Technique:** How do you spread the peanut butter evenly across the bread without tearing it? Do you apply the peanut butter first or the jelly? How do you ensure that the ingredients don't spill over the edges when you put the slices together?

4. **Assembly:** Do you press the slices together gently, or do you need to align them perfectly to avoid a mess? How do you cut the sandwich—diagonally or straight across?

Each of these steps involves decisions that can affect the outcome. Skipping or glossing over any of them can lead to a sandwich that is less than satisfying: unevenly spread, too soggy, or even inedible. The same principle applies to cybersecurity.

In cybersecurity, the consequences of superficial analysis are far more serious than a poorly made sandwich. When securing a network, every detail matters. Every step, every decision, every assumption must be examined and understood in depth. Failing to do so can leave vulnerabilities that attackers can exploit.

Consider the issue of public vs. private access to a secure network. On the surface, it might seem sufficient to protect the login page with a password or multifactor authentication (MFA). But as we will discuss in subsequent chapters, simply adding layers of security without a deep understanding of the underlying system can create a false sense of security.

For example, if the login page is publicly accessible, then no matter how strong the password or how many factors are involved in authentication, the network is still exposed to potential attacks. Hackers can attempt brute-force attacks, phishing schemes, or other exploits to gain unauthorized access. By not thoroughly analyzing the entire process, from the moment a user attempts to access the network to the final step of authentication, we miss critical points of failure that undermine the entire security framework.

Just as making a peanut butter and jelly sandwich requires careful consideration of each step, so too does securing a network. It's not enough to simply add more layers of security; we must ask the right questions and ensure that every aspect of the process is thoroughly analyzed:

- What happens when a user tries to access the network?

- How is their identity verified?

- Is the authentication process secure, or are there gaps that could be exploited?

- Does the public access point compromise the private nature of the network?

- Are we relying on superficial mitigations instead of addressing the root cause of vulnerabilities?

These questions, and many more like them, need to be asked and answered in detail. Only by doing so can we build a truly secure network that is resilient to attacks.

The peanut butter and jelly exercise is a lesson in humility. It teaches us that no matter how simple a task may seem, there is always more to it than meets the eye. In cybersecurity, this lesson is invaluable. It reminds us that we must never assume we know all the answers or that we can skip steps in the process. Instead, we must approach each challenge with the same thoroughness and attention to detail that we would use in a critical mission.

In the end, the key to effective network security is the same as the key to making a great sandwich: careful planning, detailed analysis, and an understanding that even the smallest details can have a big impact. By applying these principles, we can avoid the pitfalls of superficial analysis and build networks that are not just secure but resilient against the ever-evolving threats of the digital world.

As we saw in the analogy of making a peanut butter and jelly sandwich, assuming simplicity without considering essential details leads to flawed results. Similarly, in cybersecurity, the oversimplified approach of indirect interaction neglects critical vulnerabilities and leaves networks exposed. Direct user interaction (where the user's presence and identity are verified at each step) ensures that the network knows exactly who is accessing it and under what circumstances. This level of detail is not just a precaution; it's a necessity in a world where the stakes are as high as they are in network security.

By embracing a detailed, comprehensive approach to cybersecurity, we can build a future where networks are truly secure, not just protected by a superficial layer of defenses. This means rethinking how we interact with networks, how we verify users, and how we address the root causes of vulnerabilities rather than just their symptoms. The journey to a secure network is not unlike the process of making a perfect sandwich: it requires attention to every step, no matter how small.

With an estimated reading time of approximately 5 minutes for 1,027 words, the estimated damage cost if compromised is $95 million.

CHAPTER 3

The Science of Authentication

Authentication is the backbone of network security. It is the process by which a system verifies the identity of a user before granting access to secure resources. In theory, authentication should be a simple, binary decision: either the user is who they claim to be, or they are not. However, the reality is far more complex, particularly when the methods of authentication are built on flawed principles. This chapter explores the science behind authentication, the binary nature of computer science, and how current authentication methods fall short.

Binary Logic in Computer Science

At its core, computer science is built on binary logic. Every decision made by a computer is binary: yes or no, true or false, 0 or 1. This simplicity is what makes computers so powerful and reliable. When applied to authentication, this binary nature means that the system should unequivocally determine whether a user is authorized to access the network. There is no room for ambiguity.

© Christopher Murphy 2025
C. Murphy, *Quantum Security*, Apress Pocket Guides,
https://doi.org/10.1007/979-8-8688-1240-8_3

The Pitfalls of Indirect Interaction

However, when we examine current authentication methods, we find that they introduce a level of uncertainty that is at odds with the binary nature of computer science. This uncertainty arises primarily from the reliance on indirect interaction and the transmission of data over potentially insecure channels.

As discussed in the previous chapter, indirect interaction involves users accessing a network through a browser or installed software, which transmits data to the network for authentication. The problem with this approach is that it relies on the assumption that the data being transmitted is trustworthy and accurately represents the identity of the user.

Where Indirect Interaction Fails

This assumption is where indirect interaction fails. Data can be intercepted, manipulated, or spoofed. Cybercriminals have developed countless techniques to exploit this vulnerability, from phishing attacks that trick users into revealing their credentials to man-in-the-middle (MITM) attacks that alter the data enroute to the network. The result is an authentication process that is fundamentally flawed because it cannot guarantee the authenticity of the data it receives.

Direct Interaction: A Binary Solution

Direct interaction, on the other hand, eliminates this uncertainty. By using a digital identification (digital ID) that is directly connected to the network, the system can verify the presence and identity of the user without relying on transmitted data. This method aligns perfectly with the binary nature of computer science: either the digital ID is present and authenticated, or it is not.

Single-Factor Authentication: An Insecure Approach

One of the most significant issues in current authentication methods is the use of single-factor authentication (SFA). In SFA, only one piece of evidence is required to verify a user's identity, typically a password. This approach is inherently insecure because it relies on a single point of failure. If the password is compromised, the entire authentication process is defeated.

The Misinterpretation of Multifactor Authentication

Despite regulatory requirements and industry standards that call for multifactor authentication (MFA), systems continue to rely on SFA. This is due to a misunderstanding of what constitutes true MFA. Simply put, MFA requires the use of more than one distinct factor to verify a user's identity. These factors are typically categorized as

- **Something you know** (e.g., a password or PIN)

- **Something you have** (e.g., a security token or digital ID)

- **Something you are** (e.g., biometric verification, like a fingerprint or face scan)

The Illusion of Security in MFA Implementations

However, what is presented as MFA is, in reality, SFA in disguise. For example, a system might use a password (something you know) and a one-time code sent to a phone (which also becomes something you know once received). Both factors rely on transmitted data, which means they are essentially the same type of factor. The same is true with biometrics at a device, as this also becomes transmitted data. This fails to meet the true definition of MFA as outlined by organizations like the National Institute of Standards and Technology (NIST).

The Illusion of MFA As a Widespread Issue

The illusion of MFA is one of the most pervasive issues in cybersecurity today. Systems claim to offer MFA but fail to meet the necessary criteria. This illusion is perpetuated by the reliance on indirect interaction and the assumption that transmitted data can serve as multiple distinct factors.

Achieving True MFA with Digital IDs

For true MFA to be achieved, the authentication process must involve more than one distinct factor. This means that at least one factor must be something the user has, such as a digital ID, which is not merely data that can be intercepted or spoofed. This distinction is crucial because it ensures that the authentication process is robust and resistant to the most common types of cyberattacks.

The Dangers of Transmitted Data in Authentication

When authentication is based solely on transmitted data, it is vulnerable to a wide range of attacks. Cybercriminals intercept the data, manipulate it, or use it to impersonate legitimate users. This is why the illusion of MFA is so dangerous; it gives organizations a false sense of security while leaving them exposed to significant risks.

Binary Principles in Cybersecurity vs. Network Security

Cybersecurity and network security, though often used interchangeably, represent fundamentally different approaches to securing an organization's digital assets. To truly secure a network, authentication must adhere to the binary principles of computer science. Either the user is authenticated, or they are not. There can be no middle ground, no assumptions, and no reliance on potentially compromised data.

Digital IDs: A Paradigm Shift in Authentication

This is where the concept of direct user interaction through a digital ID comes into play. By using a digital ID that is directly connected to the network, the system can verify the user's identity without relying on transmitted data. This approach eliminates the vulnerabilities associated with indirect interaction and ensures that the authentication process is binary and unequivocal.

The Power of Binary Authentication

With direct user interaction, the authentication process becomes a simple yes-or-no decision. The digital ID is either present and authenticated, or it is not. This aligns perfectly with the binary nature of computer science and provides a level of security that is simply not possible with indirect interaction.

The Role of Digital IDs in Enabling True MFA

Digital IDs represent a paradigm shift in how authentication is performed. Unlike traditional methods that rely on passwords or transmitted data, digital IDs are tangible, serialized identifiers that are directly connected to the network. This means that they can be used to prove both the identity and presence of the user in a way that is secure and verifiable.

A Future Built on Binary Logic

When a user connects their digital ID to the network, the system can immediately verify their identity and grant access based on predefined rules and permissions. This process is not only more secure but also more efficient than traditional methods. It eliminates the risk of phishing and other attacks and ensures that only authorized users can access sensitive resources.

Ensuring Robust Security with Digital IDs

Digital IDs also enable true MFA by providing a distinct factor that is separate from transmitted data. This means that even if an attacker were to intercept data during the authentication process, they would still be unable to gain access without the physical digital ID. This is the essence of binary authentication (either the digital ID is present and authenticated, or it is not).

With an estimated reading time of approximately 6 minutes for 1,135 words, the estimated damage cost if compromised is $114 million.

CHAPTER 4

The Failure of Indirect Interaction

Interaction methods are a fundamental aspect of user access and engagement with secure networks. The early decision to allow public access through browsers, an approach we now refer to as indirect interaction, was driven by a desire for convenience and broad accessibility. However, this choice has had far-reaching consequences, many of which have proven detrimental to network security. This chapter explores the concept of indirect interaction, why it has failed to provide adequate security, and how it has led to the proliferation of cyber threats.

Understanding Indirect Interaction

Indirect interaction is a method by which users engage with a network through a browser or installed software, transmitting data over the Internet to authenticate their identity and gain access to secure resources. This approach has become the standard for both public and private online activity, primarily because it is perceived to allow for ease of access from virtually anywhere in the world.

© Christopher Murphy 2025
C. Murphy, *Quantum Security*, Apress Pocket Guides,
https://doi.org/10.1007/979-8-8688-1240-8_4

When a user accesses a secure network through a browser, they typically do so by entering a username and password on a public-facing login page. This information is then sent over the Internet to the network's servers, where it is verified against stored credentials. If the data matches, the user is granted access.

The Fundamental Flaw in Transmitted Data

However, this process is fundamentally flawed. The reliance on transmitted data means that security is only as strong as the data being sent. If that data is intercepted, guessed, or otherwise compromised, the entire security process fails. This weakness is the Achilles' heel of indirect interaction and has led to a wide array of cyber threats.

The Vulnerabilities of Indirect Interaction

1. **Phishing Attacks**: Phishing is one of the most common and effective methods used by cybercriminals to exploit indirect interaction. By tricking users into entering their credentials on a fake login page, attackers can capture the data they need to access the network. Because the interaction is indirect, the network cannot differentiate between legitimate and illegitimate login attempts until after the data has been processed, by which time the damage may already be done.

2. **Man-in-the-Middle Attacks**: In a man-in-the-middle (MITM) attack, a cybercriminal intercepts the communication between the user and the network. This allows the attacker to capture, alter,

or inject data into the interaction. Since the network relies on the transmitted data to verify the user's identity, any compromise in the data stream can lead to unauthorized access.

3. **Brute-Force Attacks**: Brute-force attacks involve systematically trying all possible combinations of a password until the correct one is found. Because indirect interaction typically relies on passwords as a primary form of authentication, these attacks can be highly effective. Even with measures like rate limiting or account lockout, determined attackers can often find ways to bypass these defenses, especially if the password is weak or commonly used.

4. **Credential Stuffing**: Credential stuffing takes advantage of the fact that many users reuse passwords across multiple sites. If a user's credentials are compromised in one breach, attackers can use those same credentials to gain access to other networks. Since indirect interaction does not inherently validate whether the person using the credentials is the legitimate owner, this type of attack is alarmingly effective.

The Issue of Assumed Identity

One of the most significant issues with indirect interaction is the concept of assumed identity. When a user logs in via a browser, the network has no way of knowing whether the person entering the credentials is the legitimate user or an impostor. The system simply assumes that if the correct data is provided, the user must be who they claim to be.

This assumption is at the heart of many security breaches. Cybercriminals have developed numerous techniques to obtain the necessary data, whether through phishing, keylogging, or social engineering, allowing them to impersonate legitimate users with ease. Once inside the network, these attackers can move laterally, accessing sensitive information and causing significant damage.

The False Sense of Security in Indirect Interaction

Indirect interaction often gives users and organizations a false sense of security. Many believe that because they use complex passwords, two-factor authentication (2FA), or encrypted communications, their interactions are secure. However, as we've seen, these measures are insufficient when the underlying method of interaction is flawed.

For instance, 2FA is commonly used to add an extra layer of security. But in an indirect interaction model, the second factor, typically a code sent via SMS or generated by an app, is still just data transmitted over the Internet. This data can be intercepted or spoofed, undermining the entire purpose of 2FA.

Limitations of Encryption in Indirect Interaction

Similarly, while encryption can protect data in transit, it does nothing to verify the legitimacy of the user sending the data. Encrypted phishing sites, for example, can appear just as secure as legitimate ones, tricking users into entering their credentials and handing them over to attackers.

The Economic Cost of Cybercrime from Indirect Interaction

The reliance on indirect interaction has led to a cybersecurity environment riddled with vulnerabilities. Breaches have become commonplace, costing companies billions of dollars in damages, lost revenue, and damaged reputation. According to estimates, cybercrime costs have exceeded $24.8 trillion in the past five years, with projections for the next five years expected to double.

Reactive Measures and a Flawed Foundation

Indirect interaction has also necessitated the development of a vast array of mitigation strategies, firewalls, intrusion detection systems, antivirus software, and more, each designed to plug the holes created by this fundamentally insecure method of access. But these measures are reactive, addressing symptoms rather than the root cause of the problem.

A Flawed Foundation for Network Security

At its core, indirect interaction is a fatally flawed foundation for network security. It was never designed with today's cybersecurity threats in mind and has been stretched beyond its limits as the Internet has evolved. The continuous patching and layering of security solutions on top of this flawed model have only added complexity without addressing the underlying issues.

The Need for Direct Interaction

The failure of indirect interaction lies in its inability to truly verify identity. When security is based on assumptions and transmitted data, it is inherently vulnerable. No matter how many layers of security are added, if the foundation is weak, the entire structure is at risk of collapse.

To move beyond the limitations of indirect interaction, a new approach is needed, one that eliminates the assumption of identity and replaces it with verifiable proof. This is where the concept of direct user interaction comes into play, offering a way to secure networks by ensuring that only authorized individuals can access them.

Direct Interaction and Digital IDs

Direct interaction, through the use of digital IDs, shifts the focus from transmitting data over potentially insecure channels to a system where the user's presence and identity are verified in real time, without reliance on data that can be intercepted or altered. This approach aligns with the binary nature of computer science, ensuring that authentication is either a yes or a no, with no room for ambiguity.

The failure of indirect interaction has been a critical factor in the rise of cyber threats since the Internet's inception. While it provided the convenience and accessibility needed in the early days of the Internet, it has proven inadequate in the face of the modern Internet and its cybersecurity challenges. To build a more secure future, we must move beyond this flawed model and embrace a new method of interaction that offers true security.

By transitioning from indirect to direct interaction, organizations can eliminate the vulnerabilities inherent in current authentication methods and establish a stronger, more resilient network security framework. This shift is not just a technological change but a fundamental rethinking of how we approach identity and access management in the digital age.

With an estimated reading time of approximately 7 minutes for 1,303 words, the estimated damage cost if compromised is $133 million.

CHAPTER 5

Digital IDs: The Solution That Was Ignored

In the early 2000s, as the Internet was rapidly expanding, the concept of digital identification (digital ID) was introduced as a promising solution for securing online activities. Digital IDs were envisioned as a robust method for authenticating users, providing a secure way to verify identity in a digital world. However, despite their potential, digital IDs were largely overlooked in favor of more convenient but less secure methods.

The Basics of Digital IDs

A digital ID is a uniquely serialized, encrypted identification assigned to a specific individual or entity. Unlike traditional authentication methods that rely on passwords or other forms of transmitted data, a digital ID is a physical token that directly connects to the network, providing a secure and verifiable proof of identity. This token is not merely data that can be intercepted or manipulated; it is a tangible item that must be present and authenticated by the network.

© Christopher Murphy 2025
C. Murphy, *Quantum Security*, Apress Pocket Guides,
https://doi.org/10.1007/979-8-8688-1240-8_5

Direct Interaction and Binary Security

The key innovation of digital IDs lies in their ability to provide direct user interaction with the network. When a user connects their digital ID, the network can immediately verify the presence and identity of the user, eliminating the dependence on passwords or other vulnerable forms of authentication. This method aligns perfectly with the binary nature of computer science; either the digital ID is present and authenticated, or it is not. The gathering of user credentials verifies ownership of the digital ID.

Early Resistance to Digital IDs

When digital IDs were first proposed as a solution for secure authentication, the Internet was in its infancy. The focus at the time was on making the Internet as accessible and user-friendly as possible. The idea of requiring a physical identification to access online services was seen as cumbersome and inconvenient. Companies were eager to attract users to their platforms, and any barrier to entry, such as a digital ID, was viewed as a potential deterrent. However, this perception was incorrect because it assumed that the company's secure network must use the same interaction method as their public network.

Technological and Cost Constraints

Additionally, the technology infrastructure required to support digital IDs was not as well-developed as it is today. Many organizations lacked the resources or expertise to implement such a system, and the cost of deploying digital IDs was seen as prohibitive. Instead of embracing this far more secure method, companies opted for less secure but more convenient alternatives, such as passwords and security questions.

Consequences of Ignoring Digital IDs

As a result, the idea of digital IDs was largely set aside in favor of methods that prioritized convenience over security. This decision, driven by short-term goals and immediate cost concerns, has had long-term consequences that continue to plague network security efforts to this day.

The Cost of Convenience Over Security

The decision to ignore digital IDs in favor of less secure methods has led to a host of network security issues. The reliance on passwords, which can be easily guessed, stolen, or phished, has resulted in countless data breaches and security incidents. Additionally, the use of transmitted data for authentication has created vulnerabilities that cybercriminals have exploited with increasing sophistication.

What Could Have Been with Digital IDs

Had digital IDs been widely adopted from the beginning, many of these issues could have been avoided. The direct user interaction provided by digital IDs would have eliminated the need for one-time codes, security questions, and other insecure forms of authentication. It would have made phishing attacks virtually impossible, as attackers would need the physical digital ID to gain access. Moreover, it would have provided a true form of multifactor authentication (MFA), aligning with regulatory requirements and significantly reducing the risk of unauthorized access.

Revisiting Digital IDs Today

Despite being overlooked in the past, digital IDs remain the only viable and effective solution for securing online activities. The technology infrastructure needed to support digital IDs is now more advanced and accessible, making it easier for organizations to implement this method. Additionally, the growing awareness of network security threats has made companies more receptive to solutions that prioritize security over convenience.

In today's digital landscape, the need for secure authentication methods is more pressing than ever. Cybercriminals have become increasingly adept at exploiting vulnerabilities in traditional authentication methods, leading to significant financial and reputational damage for organizations. Digital IDs offer a way to close these security gaps by providing a method of authentication that is both secure and verifiable.

Aligning with Regulatory Requirements

Furthermore, the use of digital IDs aligns with regulatory requirements for true MFA. As discussed in the previous chapter, MFA requires more than one distinct factor to verify a user's identity. Digital IDs provide this distinct factor, ensuring that authentication is based on something the user has, rather than just something they know. This makes digital IDs not only a secure option but also a compliant one.

The Path Forward with Digital IDs

To move forward, organizations must recognize the value of digital IDs and begin the process of integrating them into their security strategies. This requires a shift in mindset from prioritizing convenience to prioritizing security. While the initial implementation of digital IDs may require an investment of time and resources, the long-term benefits far outweigh the costs.

Protecting Digital Assets and Reducing Risk

Adopting digital IDs can help organizations protect their digital assets, comply with regulatory requirements, and reduce the risk of cyberattacks. By providing a secure method of authentication, digital IDs eliminate many of the vulnerabilities that exist in current systems and create a more robust security framework.

A Missed Opportunity with Lasting Implications

Digital IDs represent a missed opportunity in the history of cybersecurity. Had they been adopted when first introduced, many of the security challenges we face today could have been avoided. However, it is not too late to embrace this technology and realize its potential to transform the way we approach authentication.

With an estimated reading time of approximately 5 minutes for 989 words, the estimated damage cost if compromised is $95 million.

CHAPTER 6

Direct User Interaction: The Game Changer

In cybersecurity, one concept has the potential to radically transform how we protect sensitive information: direct user interaction. Unlike traditional methods that rely on indirect, browser-based interactions, direct user interaction bypasses many of the vulnerabilities that have plagued online security for decades. This chapter explores how direct user interaction, when combined with digital identification, creates a more secure environment for network access and activity. It also delves into how this approach differs from current practices and why it is a critical advancement in network security.

Understanding Direct User Interaction

Direct user interaction is a method of network access that eliminates the need for browsers or other intermediary software. Instead, it relies on a physical identification that directly connects to the network. This uniquely serialized digital identification is not merely a piece of data that can be transmitted and potentially intercepted; it is a tangible object that must be present for access to be granted.

© Christopher Murphy 2025
C. Murphy, *Quantum Security*, Apress Pocket Guides,
https://doi.org/10.1007/979-8-8688-1240-8_6

The Problem with Indirect Interaction

When a user interacts with a network through direct user interaction, they connect their digital identification directly to the network login interface. This bypasses the browser, eliminating the security risks associated with browser-based interactions. The network then authenticates the user's identity and presence with a high degree of certainty, ensuring that only authorized individuals gain access to the network.

How Direct Interaction Differs from Current Practices

To fully appreciate the impact of direct user interaction, it is essential to understand how it differs from the indirect interaction methods that are commonly used today. Indirect interaction involves the use of browsers or installed software to connect to a network. In this model, the user's credentials and other identifying information are transmitted over the Internet, where they can be intercepted, spoofed, or otherwise manipulated by malicious actors.

Indirect interaction also relies on the assumption that the data received by the network is valid and has not been tampered with. This creates a significant vulnerability, as attackers can exploit various methods to impersonate users, steal credentials, or launch other types of cyberattacks. Furthermore, indirect interaction always involves single-factor authentication, where the network relies on transmitted data rather than distinct, verifiable factors to authenticate users.

The Advantages of Direct User Interaction

Direct user interaction, on the other hand, eliminates these vulnerabilities by removing the intermediary software and connecting the user directly to the network. With direct interaction, the user's digital identification is the primary factor used for authentication. This identification cannot be intercepted or spoofed because it is a physical object that must be present for the interaction to occur. As a result, the network can verify the user's identity and presence with far greater accuracy and security.

Key Benefits of Direct User Interaction

The shift to direct user interaction offers numerous benefits for network security, making it a game changer in the field of cybersecurity. Some of the most significant advantages include the following:

1. **Enhanced Security**: By eliminating the browser and other intermediaries, direct user interaction removes a major attack surface for cybercriminals. The use of digital identification ensures that only authorized users can access the network login, eliminating the risk of unauthorized access, phishing attacks, and other forms of cybercrime.

2. **True Multifactor Authentication (MFA)**: Direct user interaction allows for the implementation of true MFA, as defined by regulatory bodies like the Federal Financial Institutions Examination Council (FFIEC). The digital identification serves as a distinct factor that is separate from any data transmitted over the network. This ensures that authentication is based on more than just transmitted data, meeting the requirements for true MFA.

3. **Reduced Reliance on Mitigations**: With direct user interaction, many of the mitigation solutions currently used to secure browser-based interactions become unnecessary. For example, there is no need for IP whitelisting, CAPTCHA, and other forms of secondary authentication because the primary authentication method is already secure.

4. **Improved User Experience**: While security is often seen as being at odds with convenience, direct user interaction enhances the user experience. By streamlining the authentication process and reducing the need for additional security checks, users can access the network more quickly and efficiently.

5. **Compliance and Futureproofing**: As regulatory bodies continue to tighten security requirements, direct user interaction offers a way to stay ahead of the curve. By adopting this method, organizations can ensure compliance with current and future regulations, reducing the risk of fines and other penalties.

Overcoming Challenges and Resistance

While the benefits of direct user interaction are clear, implementing this approach comes with minimal challenges. Yet, preconceptions have proven a more difficult challenge to overcome. Organizations must be willing to invest in digital identifications. This investment is minimal and targeted, requiring no change to existing infrastructure or procedures. However, the minor expense is far outweighed by the long-term security and efficiency gains.

Additionally, there may be resistance to change, especially in organizations that have relied on traditional cybersecurity methods for many years. Education and awareness are key to overcoming this resistance, as stakeholders need to understand the limitations of current methods and the advantages of direct user interaction.

A Paradigm Shift in Cybersecurity

Direct user interaction represents a paradigm shift in how we approach network security. By eliminating the browser and other intermediary software, this method offers a more secure, efficient, and compliant way to authenticate users and protect sensitive information. As cyber threats continue to evolve, the need for innovative solutions like direct user interaction will only become more pressing.

Binary Authentication and the Future of Security

This game-changing approach not only addresses the fundamental weaknesses of indirect interaction but also aligns with the binary nature of computer science, where security is a clear, unequivocal process. By adopting direct user interaction, organizations can move beyond the flawed security models of the past and embrace a future where network access is both secure and seamless.

With an estimated reading time of approximately 5 minutes for 972 words, the estimated damage cost if compromised is $95 million.

CHAPTER 7

Digital Superposition: A New Layer in Network Security

In the world of quantum physics, the concept of superposition allows a particle to exist in multiple states until it is observed, at which point it collapses into one definite state. This principle has fascinating parallels in the realm of network security, particularly when applied to digital identification (digital ID). A user's presence or absence on a network, represented by a digital ID, can be queried at any moment. Until this query is made, the user's state remains indeterminate. Once verification occurs, the digital ID collapses into a single truth: the user is either present or absent on the network.

Quantum Superposition and Network Security

Much like quantum superposition, where observation defines the particle's state, the request for a digital ID's existence determines whether an individual is interacting with the network. This concept is not just theoretical; it has been proven and represents a significant shift in how

© Christopher Murphy 2025
C. Murphy, *Quantum Security*, Apress Pocket Guides,
https://doi.org/10.1007/979-8-8688-1240-8_7

we approach security. The digital ID functions as a distinct authentication factor, providing tangible proof that an authorized user is physically connected to the network, thereby eliminating risks associated with impersonation and fraud. This direct assertion collapses all potential security threats related to identity down to a simple binary question: is this specific individual present?

The Vulnerabilities of Indirect Interaction

In traditional cybersecurity architecture, a user's identity is represented by transmitted data, data that can be intercepted, altered, or replicated. This method of indirect interaction leaves networks vulnerable to various forms of attack, including phishing, man-in-the-middle attacks, and credential theft. Digital IDs, however, introduce a new paradigm by establishing a user's superposition on the World Wide Web. A user's identity is tied directly to the digital ID, and when the ID is connected, it initiates a private, secure interface. There is no ambiguity. When disconnected, the ID no longer interacts with the network, leaving no traces behind on local devices and further securing the interaction. This approach effectively shifts the endpoint from the local device to the ID itself.

Proving Presence and Absence

This model also addresses a significant gap in cybersecurity: proving user absence. Traditional security systems focus on verifying presence but rarely address the importance of confirming that a user is *not* present. By verifying that a specific user is absent, the network can prevent unauthorized access and thwart attacks that rely on impersonation or stolen credentials. In essence, presence ensures trust in user actions, while absence ensures that any unapproved action is immediately halted.

Greater Control Over Secure Activities

For organizations, this shift in identity management from indirect to direct interaction offers unparalleled control over secure activities. It becomes virtually impossible for unauthorized users to gain access or perform actions without the network first verifying their digital existence. The digital ID does not just verify credentials; it verifies the physical presence of the user, ensuring that the person taking action is the same person who holds the digital ID, has connected it to a device, and has logged into the network.

Enhancing Security Architecture

Proving user existence through a digital ID enhances every other element of security architecture. It operates concurrently with all existing systems and requires only slight modifications, such as the introduction of a new authorized user access point and the deployment of digital IDs to authorized employees. This innovative use of superposition in digital authentication marks a turning point in network security, providing both greater flexibility and uncompromising protection.

The Profound Implications of Digital Superposition

The implications of applying digital superposition to network security are profound. By leveraging the principles of quantum superposition, digital IDs offer a robust solution to the challenges posed by indirect interaction and data transmission. They ensure that every interaction is verifiable, secure, and tied directly to the individual, rather than to vulnerable data streams. This approach not only strengthens security but also simplifies the authentication process, reducing the burden on users and administrators alike.

A New Layer of Network Security

In this new layer of network security, digital IDs represent the next step in the evolution of authentication. They provide a clear, binary response to the question of user presence, eliminating ambiguity and greatly reducing the risk of unauthorized access. As organizations continue to face increasingly sophisticated cyber threats, the adoption of digital superposition through digital IDs will become essential for ensuring the integrity and security of network interactions.

Redefining Security Through Digital Superposition

By integrating the principles of quantum physics into digital authentication, we are not just enhancing security; we are redefining it. The ability to prove both presence and absence in a secure, verifiable manner represents a significant advancement in network security, one that will shape the future of how we protect and manage digital identities.

With an estimated reading time of approximately 4 minutes for 787 words, the estimated damage cost if compromised is $76 million.

CHAPTER 8

Rethinking Security: Insights from Einstein and Hawking

Before diving into the technical aspects of cybersecurity, we must pause and reflect on a critical oversight: the fundamental assumptions that have guided our security decisions for decades. Two renowned thinkers, Albert Einstein and Stephen Hawking, provide timeless insights that help expose the root cause of persistent failures in network security. Their wisdom challenges us to rethink our approach to cybersecurity from both a philosophical and practical standpoint, urging us to break free from outdated paradigms and embrace innovative solutions.

Einstein's Wisdom: Rethinking Our Approach

> *We cannot solve our problems with the same thinking we used when we created them.*

> —Albert Einstein

© Christopher Murphy 2025
C. Murphy, *Quantum Security*, Apress Pocket Guides,
https://doi.org/10.1007/979-8-8688-1240-8_8

This quote encapsulates the dilemma of modern cybersecurity. The Internet was created with a focus on open access, information sharing, and convenience, not security. This architecture, designed for openness, has been retrofitted to protect private, sensitive information, leading to a fundamental conflict between its original purpose and the demands of security.

The same architecture that invites public interaction has been leveraged to protect private, sensitive information, resulting in an inherently flawed system. The underlying design flaw, allowing public access to secure content, has led to layer upon layer of mitigation, each attempting to address the symptoms rather than the root cause. The result is a patchwork of security measures that are reactive, complex, and ultimately inadequate.

The Flaw of Traditional Security Models

Einstein's perspective encourages us to rethink security protocols from the ground up, to question whether we're truly protecting networks or merely adding Band-Aids to problems created by outdated assumptions. His insight urges us to move beyond the limitations of traditional security models and explore new paradigms that align with the original purpose of the Internet while also addressing its current security needs.

Instead of attempting to patch flawed systems, we must shift to new paradigms like direct user interaction and digital identification. These approaches directly challenge the status quo by removing the public access point from secure networks, thereby reducing the attack surface and eliminating the need for many of the mitigation strategies that have become standard practice.

Hawking's Insight: The Illusion of Knowledge

The greatest enemy of knowledge is not ignorance; it is the illusion of knowledge.

—Stephen Hawking

Hawking's words warn us of the dangers of assuming we know more than we actually do. In cybersecurity, many solutions give the illusion of safety without addressing the fundamental vulnerabilities they claim to protect against.

Take, for instance, multifactor authentication (MFA), which is often portrayed as a bulletproof solution. While MFA adds a layer of security, it relies on indirect interaction and transmitted data, components that are inherently vulnerable due to their exposure to the public Internet. The illusion that MFA alone can prevent identity theft and unauthorized access has allowed cybersecurity professionals to overlook more profound, systemic flaws in network security.

The Illusion of Security in Modern Systems

Hawking's insight reminds us that if our security measures are built on illusions, then our networks are far more vulnerable than we would like to believe. The complacency bred by these illusions can lead to catastrophic consequences, as attackers exploit the gaps left by these so-called secure measures.

To address this, we must focus on ensuring that security is built on verifiable, tangible factors. This is where digital ID technology comes into play. By tying authentication directly to the user's physical presence and identity, digital IDs eliminate the guesswork involved in indirect methods and provide a level of security that is both practical and philosophically sound.

45

Reevaluating the Foundation of Cybersecurity

Incorporating the wisdom of both Einstein and Hawking into cybersecurity calls for a fundamental shift in how we think about and approach network security. Rather than continually building and rebuilding on the same flawed foundation, we must redefine the parameters of secure access. This involves the following:

1. **Reevaluating the Foundation of Cybersecurity**: Just as Einstein's theory of relativity required a reevaluation of the fundamental laws of physics, so too must we reevaluate the foundational assumptions of cybersecurity. This means questioning the reliance on public-facing systems for private, sensitive interactions and considering how the architecture of the Internet itself may need to evolve.

2. **Embracing Innovation and Disruption**: As Hawking's work challenged existing scientific paradigms, so must we challenge the prevailing cybersecurity models. This includes embracing disruptive technologies like digital IDs, which provide a clear, verifiable link between the user and their actions on the network, without relying on easily compromised transmitted data.

3. **Shifting from Reactive to Proactive Security**: Both Einstein and Hawking emphasized the importance of forward-thinking and anticipating future challenges. In cybersecurity, this means moving away from reactive mitigation strategies

and toward proactive prevention, where the focus is on eliminating vulnerabilities *before* they can be exploited.

4. **Building Security on Immutable Truths**: The concept of digital IDs ties directly into Hawking's warning about the illusion of knowledge. By ensuring that authentication is based on immutable, verifiable factors, such as the physical presence of a digital ID, we move away from the illusion of security and toward a system that is grounded in reality.

Moving Beyond Illusions to True Security

The insights of Einstein and Hawking compel us to rethink not just the tools and techniques we use in cybersecurity, but the very principles on which those tools are built. As we move forward, it is essential to recognize that true security cannot be achieved by simply layering more defenses onto a flawed system. Instead, we must be willing to challenge the assumptions that have guided us thus far and embrace new, innovative solutions that address the root cause of our vulnerabilities.

The Future of Cybersecurity with Digital IDs

Digital IDs and direct user interaction represent the embodiment of this new approach. By focusing on private user interaction, eliminating public access to sensitive content, and proving identity in a way that is both verifiable and immutable, we can create a security model that is not only more effective but also more aligned with the realities of the digital world.

The Paradigm Shift in Cybersecurity

As we stand at this crossroads, the choice is clear: continue down the path of incremental improvements and reactive mitigations, or embrace the paradigm shift that Einstein and Hawking's insights demand. The future of cybersecurity depends on our willingness to rethink our approach, to question our assumptions, and to build a new foundation that is capable of withstanding the challenges of tomorrow.

With an estimated reading time of approximately 5 minutes for 1,071 words, the estimated damage cost if compromised is $95 million

CHAPTER 9

The Power of Absence: Proving What Isn't There

In network security, the focus is typically on proving presence, verifying that an authorized user is interacting with the system. However, equally critical is the ability to prove absence, the capacity to confirm when an authorized user is not present. This seemingly simple concept holds profound implications for preventing many of today's most damaging cyber exploits, such as Florida's Oldsmar Water Plant hack and the infamous SolarWinds breach.

Shifting the Focus: Proving Absence

Proving absence is not just about adding another layer of security; it fundamentally shifts how we approach the concept of user verification. When networks can definitively prove that a specific user is not present, they close the door on a wide range of cyber threats that rely on the exploitation of assumed presence. This chapter explores the significance of absence in network security, how it can be leveraged to prevent attacks, and the broader implications of this often-overlooked concept.

© Christopher Murphy 2025
C. Murphy, *Quantum Security*, Apress Pocket Guides,
https://doi.org/10.1007/979-8-8688-1240-8_9

The Importance of Proving Absence

The power of absence lies in its ability to prevent unauthorized access before it even begins. In traditional network security models, presence is verified through various means, passwords, biometrics, or multifactor authentication (MFA). However, these methods all operate on the assumption that presence equals authenticity. If a user is present and verified, they are granted access. But what happens when an attacker gains access to the credentials or methods that verify presence? This is where absence becomes a critical factor.

Turning the Tables on Cyberattackers

When a network can verify that an authorized user is not present, it can automatically reject any access attempts made in that user's name. This capability turns the tables on attackers, making it significantly more difficult for them to exploit stolen credentials or engage in impersonation. In essence, proving absence acts as a fail-safe that can prevent breaches even when other security measures have been compromised.

Real-World Implications of Proving Absence

The concept of proving absence is not just theoretical; it has real-world implications with the potential to prevent significant security breaches. Two high-profile incidents, the Oldsmar Water Plant hack and the SolarWinds breach, illustrate the critical need for this capability.

Case Study: The Oldsmar Water Plant Hack

In February 2021, attackers remotely accessed the control systems of a water treatment plant in Oldsmar, Florida, and attempted to increase the levels of sodium hydroxide in the water supply to dangerous levels. The attack was only thwarted because a plant operator noticed the changes and immediately reversed them. However, the attack could have been entirely prevented if the network had been able to prove the absence of the authorized user.

Had the Oldsmar Water Plant's network been able to verify that the operator's digital ID was not present at the time of the unauthorized access, the system could have automatically blocked the attack. This would have prevented the attackers from making any changes to the water treatment settings, effectively neutralizing the threat before it could escalate.

Case Study: The SolarWinds Breach

The SolarWinds breach, one of the most significant cyber incidents in recent history, involved attackers compromising the software supply chain of SolarWinds and inserting malicious code into a software update. This code allowed the attackers to gain unauthorized access to numerous government and private sector networks.

One of the key vulnerabilities exploited in the SolarWinds breach was the network's inability to confirm when legitimate users were absent. By assuming the presence of legitimate users, the compromised networks inadvertently allowed attackers to move laterally within the systems, accessing sensitive information and installing further backdoors.

If the affected networks had implemented a system capable of proving absence, the attackers' movements could have been detected and blocked. For example, if the network could verify that a specific administrator's digital ID was not present during an unusual access attempt, it could have flagged the activity as suspicious and initiated a security response. This proactive approach would have limited the attackers' ability to exploit the network, potentially preventing the breach from escalating to the level it did.

Digital IDs and the Ability to Prove Absence

The ability to prove absence hinges on the use of digital IDs, uniquely serialized and encrypted identifications assigned to specific individuals. When these digital IDs are connected to the network, they create a secure, verifiable link between the user and the network. However, the true power of digital IDs lies in their ability to be verified not just when they are present, but also when they are absent.

When a digital ID is not connected to the network, any attempts to access the network attempting to represent that ID would be automatically rejected. This ensures that only legitimate, present users can interact with the system. If an attacker attempts to use stolen credentials or a compromised device to gain access, the network can immediately detect that the corresponding digital ID is absent and block the access attempt.

Real-Time Verification for Enhanced Security

This process requires real-time verification and continuous monitoring of digital IDs, but it provides a level of security that is unmatched by traditional methods. By focusing on absence as well as presence, networks can create a more comprehensive security framework that addresses the full spectrum of potential threats.

The Future of Network Security: Proactive Prevention

The ability to prove absence has far-reaching implications for network security. It represents a shift from reactive to proactive security measures, where threats are stopped before they can cause harm. This approach also aligns with the binary nature of computer science, where security decisions should be clear and unequivocal: either the user is present, or they are not.

Simplifying Security and Reducing Reliance on Mitigations

Incorporating absence into the security equation also reduces the reliance on mitigation strategies that are often used to address the vulnerabilities of traditional authentication methods. For example, the need for constant monitoring, complex password policies, and multi-layered defenses can be minimized when the network can confidently verify the presence or absence of authorized users. This simplification not only enhances security but also reduces the complexity and cost of maintaining secure networks.

A Game Changer in Cybersecurity

The power of absence is a game-changing concept in network security, offering a new way to prevent cyber threats before they can manifest. By leveraging digital IDs and direct user interaction, networks can verify not only who is present but also who is not, closing the door on a wide range of cyber exploits.

The Path Forward: Embracing the Power of Absence

As demonstrated by the Oldsmar Water Plant hack and the SolarWinds breach, the inability to prove absence has allowed attackers to exploit networks with devastating consequences. Moving forward, the adoption of digital IDs and the ability to verify absence in real time will be critical for organizations seeking to protect their digital assets from increasingly sophisticated threats.

In the world of network security, proving what isn't there is just as important as proving what is. By embracing this concept, organizations can build a more secure, resilient, and proactive approach to safeguarding their networks against the ever-evolving landscape of cyber threats.

With an estimated reading time of approximately 6 minutes for 1,181 words, the estimated damage cost if compromised is $114 million.

CHAPTER 10

The Illusion of MFA Compliance

Multifactor authentication (MFA) is widely regarded as a cornerstone of modern cybersecurity. It promises to add layers of security by requiring multiple forms of verification before granting access to sensitive systems and data. However, the reality of MFA implementation falls short of this promise. Unfortunately what is being marketed as MFA is, in fact, nothing more than glorified single-factor authentication (SFA) disguised under a different name. This chapter will dissect the illusion of MFA compliance, examining how and why the cybersecurity industry has misrepresented true MFA and the consequences of this widespread deception.

Core Concept of MFA

At its core, MFA is designed to ensure that access to a network or system is only granted after two or more distinct factors have been verified. These factors typically fall into three categories:

1. **Something You Know**: A password or PIN

2. **Something You Have**: A physical token, smart card, or mobile device

3. **Something You Are**: Biometric data, such as fingerprints or facial recognition

© Christopher Murphy 2025
C. Murphy, *Quantum Security*, Apress Pocket Guides,
https://doi.org/10.1007/979-8-8688-1240-8_10

The idea behind MFA is that even if one factor is compromised, the others can still provide a safeguard, making unauthorized access significantly more difficult. True MFA is supposed to provide a robust, multi-layered defense against unauthorized access by requiring more than one method of verification from different categories.

Transmission of Data and Security Failures

Despite the clear definition of MFA, implementation falls short of meeting these standards. The common failure lies in the reliance on transmitted data for authentication. Whether it's a password, a one-time code sent to a mobile device, or biometric data transmitted over the Internet, these factors are all reduced to data that is sent from the user's device to the authentication server.

Once these factors are transmitted, they are no longer distinct; they are simply data that can be intercepted, manipulated, or replayed by attackers. This reduces the process to single-factor authentication (SFA), as the network is effectively only verifying one type of input: transmitted data.

Marketing of MFA Solutions

This misrepresentation is further compounded by the marketing practices of cybersecurity vendors, who claim that their solutions provide true MFA when they do not. These vendors emphasize the number of steps involved in the authentication process rather than the distinctiveness of the factors being used. As a result, organizations are led to believe they are securing their networks with MFA when, in fact, they are not.

Regulatory and Standards Violations

The failure to implement true MFA is not just a technical oversight; it's a violation of regulatory standards. Regulatory bodies, such as the National Institute of Standards and Technology (NIST) and the Federal Financial Institutions Examination Council (FFIEC), have clearly defined what constitutes true MFA. These standards require the use of more than one distinct factor from different categories. Simply using multiple data points, no matter how they are gathered or transmitted, does not meet these requirements.

In 2006, the FFIEC specifically addressed this issue by stating, "By definition, true multifactor authentication requires the use of solutions from two or more of the three categories of factors. Using multiple solutions from the same category [such as transmitted data] at different points in the process may be part of a layered security or other compensating control approach, but it would not constitute multifactor authentication." This statement underscores the importance of distinct, verifiable factors in the authentication process.

Security Risks of Misrepresented MFA

The widespread misrepresentation of MFA has serious consequences. Organizations that believe they are complying with MFA regulations are, in fact, leaving their networks vulnerable to attack. When MFA is reduced to single-factor authentication, it fails to provide the additional security layers that are supposed to protect against unauthorized access.

This vulnerability is exploited by attackers who use phishing, man-in-the-middle attacks, and other techniques to intercept and manipulate the data being transmitted during the authentication process. Once they have access to this data, they can easily bypass the so-called MFA and gain unauthorized access to the network.

Furthermore, this misrepresentation undermines trust in the cybersecurity industry. When organizations discover that their supposedly secure MFA solutions are, in fact, inadequate SFA, it erodes confidence in these vendors and the industry as a whole. This lack of trust can have far-reaching implications, from increased regulatory scrutiny to financial penalties and reputational damage.

Implementing True MFA

To protect against these vulnerabilities, it is essential that organizations implement true MFA, as defined by regulatory standards. This means using distinct factors that cannot be reduced to transmitted data alone. For example, a digital identification that directly connects to the network and requires physical presence, combined with a biometric factor that is verified locally on the device and transmitted as data, would meet the requirements for true MFA.

True MFA Provides Several Key Benefits

1. **Enhanced Security**: By requiring multiple, distinct factors, true MFA makes it significantly more difficult for attackers to gain unauthorized access. Even if one factor is compromised, the others still provide a barrier to entry.

2. **Regulatory Compliance**: Implementing true MFA ensures that organizations comply with regulatory standards, reducing the risk of fines, penalties, and other legal consequences.

3. **Increased Trust**: By using true MFA, organizations can demonstrate their commitment to security, building trust with customers, partners, and regulators.

Transitioning to True MFA

To move forward, organizations must first acknowledge the shortcomings of their current MFA implementations. This requires a critical examination of the factors being used in the authentication process and an honest assessment of whether these factors truly meet the definition of MFA.

From there, organizations can begin to implement true MFA solutions. This may involve adopting new technologies, such as digital identifications and direct user interaction, that provide distinct, verifiable factors for authentication. It may also require changes to internal processes and a shift in mindset from prioritizing convenience to prioritizing security.

The cybersecurity industry must also take responsibility for the role it has played in perpetuating the illusion of MFA compliance. Vendors must be transparent about the capabilities of their solutions and ensure that they meet regulatory standards. Only by doing so can they restore trust and provide the level of security that organizations need to protect their networks.

The illusion of MFA compliance has left organizations vulnerable to attack, believing they are secure when they are not. By understanding the true definition of MFA and implementing a solution that meets these standards, organizations can protect their networks from the growing threats they face. Direct user interaction and digital identifications represent the future of secure authentication, offering a path forward that aligns with both regulatory requirements and the realities of today's cybersecurity battlefield.

With an estimated reading time of approximately 6 minutes for 1,100 words, the estimated damage cost if compromised is $114 million.

CHAPTER 11

Pre-authentication vs. Post-authentication in Network Security

In cybersecurity, the distinction between pre-authentication and post-authentication protocols is critical. Understanding when and how security measures are applied can mean the difference between a secure network and one that is vulnerable to exploitation. Both approaches have their place in network security, but the advantages of a proactive, pre-authentication strategy, especially when combined with digital IDs and direct user interaction, are becoming increasingly evident.

Pre-authentication: A Proactive Approach

Pre-authentication involves verifying a user's identity before they are allowed to interact with the network. In this method, security protocols are initiated even before a login page is presented. Pre-authentication places access control at the very front of the security process, ensuring that only authorized users can access sensitive data or secure areas of a company's network.

© Christopher Murphy 2025
C. Murphy, *Quantum Security*, Apress Pocket Guides,
https://doi.org/10.1007/979-8-8688-1240-8_11

The Role of Digital IDs in Pre-authentication

This is where digital IDs and direct user interaction play a pivotal role. Employees are issued a uniquely serialized digital ID linked to their personal identity. When they attempt to access the network, they are required to connect this digital ID, which is then verified before the network login page becomes available. Access control, including role-based access control (RBAC), is enforced at this stage, limiting access to specific areas of the network based on the employee's role.

The Advantages of Pre-authentication

The beauty of pre-authentication lies in its proactive nature. It stops unauthorized users from ever reaching the login page, reducing the risk of unauthorized access. When credentials are provided after pre-authentication, they are always matched to the specific digital ID in a one-to-one relationship, making identity theft or impersonation virtually impossible.

Post-authentication: Reactive Security Measures

In traditional post-authentication protocols, security measures are applied after a user has been granted access to the network. In this model, users submit their login credentials first, and then security systems kick in to verify their identity. While this model can prevent unauthorized actions after a user has accessed the system, it is inherently reactive. It allows unauthorized users to interact with the network, however briefly, before their actions are flagged.

The Limitations of Post-authentication in Modern Cybersecurity

Post-authentication focuses on mitigation rather than prevention. Firewalls, encryption, and intrusion detection systems all play a role in protecting the network after a connection has been established. While these measures are necessary, they are not foolproof. In cases where an attacker gains access using compromised credentials, post-authentication systems are often too slow to stop them from causing significant damage.

In a world where phishing, identity theft, and brute-force attacks are commonplace, post-authentication methods are increasingly ineffective. These protocols allow attackers to breach networks by submitting compromised credentials and interacting with the network in real time. Once an attacker is inside, post-authentication systems must scramble to detect and mitigate the damage.

Post-authentication also relies heavily on layers of security that attempt to manage an attack rather than prevent it. By the time the attack is discovered, it is already too late. This is where post-authentication falls short, as it prioritizes damage control over prevention. The delayed response can result in significant breaches, as seen in numerous high-profile cybersecurity incidents.

The Game-Changing Potential of Pre-authentication

Pre-authentication changes the game. With digital IDs and direct user interaction, the network does not allow any interaction until identity has been proven and verified. Employees connect their digital ID to initiate the network connection, and their identity is authenticated before any credentials are entered. This virtually eliminates the possibility of phishing or identity theft because unauthorized users are blocked from accessing the system at the point of entry.

This proactive approach shifts the entire security framework from a reactive to a preventive model. Digital IDs provide a layer of identity verification that ensures only authorized individuals are allowed to interact with the network, effectively eliminating many of the vulnerabilities found in post-authentication systems.

Key Benefits of Pre-authentication with Digital IDs

The implementation of pre-authentication with digital IDs offers several key advantages:

1. **Prevention of Unauthorized Access**: By verifying identity before any interaction occurs, pre-authentication stops unauthorized users from accessing the network at the earliest possible stage. This reduces the risk of breaches and ensures that only legitimate users gain access.

2. **Protection Against Phishing and Social Engineering**: Since the digital ID is required before any login page is presented, phishing attacks that rely on tricking users into entering their credentials on fake pages become far less effective. Attackers are not presented a login interface without the correct digital ID.

3. **Elimination of Credential-Based Attacks**: Credential-based attacks, such as brute-force or credential stuffing, are rendered ineffective when pre-authentication is in place. Even if an attacker obtains valid credentials, they cannot access the network without the corresponding digital ID.

4. **Streamlined Access Control**: Pre-authentication integrates seamlessly with role-based access control systems, ensuring that users are only granted access to the areas of the network that are relevant to their role. This limits the potential damage in case of a breach and provides an additional layer of security.

5. **Compliance with Regulatory Requirements**: Pre-authentication with digital IDs helps organizations comply with stringent regulatory requirements for authentication and access control. By implementing a proactive security model, organizations can demonstrate their commitment to protecting sensitive data and maintaining the integrity of their networks.

A Paradigm Shift in Network Security

As cyber threats continue to evolve, the limitations of post-authentication methods become increasingly apparent. To build more secure networks, organizations must embrace pre-authentication with digital IDs and direct user interaction. This approach not only enhances security but also aligns with the binary nature of computer science, where access is granted based on clear, verifiable proof of identity.

By shifting from a reactive to a proactive security model, organizations can significantly reduce their risk of cyberattacks and protect their digital assets more effectively. Pre-authentication represents a critical advancement in network security, offering a robust defense against the increasingly sophisticated tactics employed by cybercriminals.

In conclusion, the integration of pre-authentication protocols with digital IDs offers a powerful solution to the inherent vulnerabilities of post-authentication methods. This shift in approach is essential for any organization seeking to secure its network against modern cyber threats, ensuring that only authorized users gain access and that unauthorized attempts are stopped before they begin.

With an estimated reading time of approximately 5 minutes for 1,041 words, the estimated damage cost if compromised is $95 million.

CHAPTER 12

Digital ID: Transforming Key Industries

While industries like healthcare and financial services have made strides in improving digital security, they remain vulnerable due to their reliance on outdated authentication methods. Digital IDs and direct user interaction represent the solution these sectors need to meet stringent security standards like HIPAA and the FFIEC regulations while addressing inherent vulnerabilities in the current infrastructure. This chapter delves deeper into how digital IDs would not only bring these industries into compliance but also revolutionize how they secure sensitive data.

Financial Services and Regulatory Compliance

Financial services are the backbone of the global economy, processing trillions of dollars daily. The FFIEC, which regulates financial institutions in the United States, has mandated multifactor authentication (MFA) for over two decades. Yet, these institutions continue to use outdated, compromised methods. Digital IDs would finally bring this sector into real compliance by proving both identity and presence.

© Christopher Murphy 2025
C. Murphy, *Quantum Security*, Apress Pocket Guides,
https://doi.org/10.1007/979-8-8688-1240-8_12

Imagine a customer holding a physical digital ID, a unique, serialized identification for online transactions (an upgraded debit card). The digital ID auto-connects to the bank's network, instantly verifying that the cardholder is present and authorized. The bank can confidently process transactions knowing the correct person is on the network, and any fraud attempts would be instantly halted by the absence of this digital ID.

With digital IDs, public access to online banking services would no longer be required, as only authorized customers could log in. This would eliminate one of the largest attack vectors for identity theft and online fraud, vastly improving the security landscape for financial institutions.

Healthcare and HIPAA Compliance

The healthcare industry has long struggled with maintaining HIPAA compliance in the digital age. Like financial services, healthcare organizations rely on public access to login systems, putting sensitive patient data at risk. A digital ID for every healthcare professional would transform this landscape by providing direct, private access to patient data. There would be no need for third-party software and, thus, no risk of unauthorized access.

The digital ID does more than prove the identity of healthcare professionals; it ensures they are physically present, reducing risks of data breaches, especially in large hospitals and research facilities. Digital IDs tied directly to each authorized user would also create an audit trail, making it easy to track who accessed patient data, when, and from where, further ensuring compliance.

In an industry where the confidentiality of patient information is paramount, digital IDs offer a solution that not only secures data but also streamlines the compliance process, making it easier for healthcare organizations to meet regulatory requirements.

Government and National Security

Endorsements were provided by military and intelligence personnel who, from 2010 to 2014, were given the opportunity to evaluate digital ID technology. As described by a former Naval Research Laboratory commander, digital ID technology was proven superior to the dual-authentication models used today, which have repeatedly failed. Had digital ID technology been adopted over a decade ago, many of the breaches that have plagued critical intelligence agencies would have been avoided.

Government agencies face the highest stakes in cybersecurity, where the failure to protect sensitive data can compromise national security. The introduction of digital IDs could protect top-secret data by ensuring only authorized personnel access secure networks. The US government's failure to adopt digital ID technology resulted in critical breaches, such as the infamous SolarWinds hack. By introducing digital IDs, agencies could lock down access to networks, rendering threats like phishing, impersonation, and brute-force attacks obsolete.

In an era where national security is increasingly dependent on cybersecurity, digital IDs offer a means to protect the most sensitive information, ensuring that only those with the proper credentials and physical presence can access critical systems.

Critical Infrastructure: Protecting Public Safety

As society becomes more reliant on technology, critical infrastructure, such as power plants, water supplies, and transportation systems, becomes more vulnerable. The Oldsmar, Florida, water plant attack in 2021, where a hacker attempted to poison the water supply, demonstrated the terrifying potential of weak cybersecurity in critical systems.

Had digital IDs been in place at Oldsmar, the attack could have been prevented entirely. Digital IDs would have verified whether an authorized employee was present before allowing any changes to the system. Any unauthorized access would have been blocked, rendering the hack impossible. This use case illustrates the potential of digital ID technology to protect critical infrastructure from increasingly sophisticated cyberattacks.

As critical infrastructure continues to be a target for cyber threats, the need for robust security measures like digital IDs becomes more pressing. Protecting these systems is not just about securing data; it's about safeguarding public safety and national security.

The Cost of Ignoring Digital ID Technology

As highlighted in the endorsement above, the decision to overlook digital ID technology in favor of less secure methods is a stark reminder of the industry's reluctance to adopt true innovation. Despite evidence that digital IDs could have significantly improved national security, the Department of Defense chose the more familiar, yet weaker, dual-authentication model. The result? Numerous data breaches that could have been avoided.

Today, the cybersecurity landscape is no different. Despite overwhelming evidence that digital IDs offer unparalleled security, the industry continues to rely on public logins and single-factor authentication, leaving networks exposed to attack.

The reluctance to adopt digital ID technology has had far-reaching consequences. From financial losses to compromised national security, the cost of ignoring this solution is staggering. It's time for industries to recognize the missed opportunity and take the necessary steps to implement digital IDs.

A New Era in Security Across Industries

Digital IDs and direct user interaction technology represent the future of network security across all industries. Whether it's protecting financial assets, healthcare data, or national secrets, this technology offers the security solution the world has been waiting for. As we've seen, the stakes are high, and the consequences of inaction are severe. It's time for industries across the board to embrace digital IDs and the transformation they bring to network security.

The adoption of digital IDs is not just about compliance or security; it's about ensuring the integrity of critical systems that society depends on. By implementing digital IDs, industries can protect their assets, meet regulatory requirements, and safeguard the future. The evidence is clear; digital IDs are the solution that can transform the way we approach cybersecurity, and the time to act is now.

With an estimated reading time of approximately 5 minutes for 1,057 words, the estimated damage cost if compromised is $96 million.

CHAPTER 13

The Mitigations That No Longer Matter

In cybersecurity, mitigation strategies have long been deployed to manage risks and protect networks from breaches. These strategies range from firewalls and intrusion detection systems to complex encryption methods and multi-layered authentication processes. However, as ineffective as these solutions have been historically, the advent of digital identifications and direct user interaction has fundamentally changed the game. Many traditional mitigation strategies are now either redundant or completely irrelevant. This chapter explores the specific mitigation techniques that are rendered obsolete by the deployment of digital IDs and direct user interaction.

The Role of Mitigation in Cybersecurity

Before diving into the specific mitigations that no longer matter, it's important to understand the role of mitigation in cybersecurity. Mitigation strategies are designed to reduce the impact of potential security threats. They do not address the source of the problem but instead layer protections to minimize damage when a breach occurs.

© Christopher Murphy 2025
C. Murphy, *Quantum Security*, Apress Pocket Guides,
https://doi.org/10.1007/979-8-8688-1240-8_13

Historically, these layers have been necessary due to inherent vulnerabilities in the systems they protect. Public access to secure network logins, indirect user interaction, and reliance on transmitted data for authentication have all created opportunities for exploitation. Mitigation strategies have been the cybersecurity industry's response to these vulnerabilities.

The introduction of digital IDs and direct user interaction represents a shift from reactive security measures to proactive prevention. This technology addresses the root cause of many security vulnerabilities, eliminating the need for extensive mitigation. When unauthorized access can be prevented at the very first point of contact, before a login page is even presented, many traditional security measures designed to protect networks from breaches that should never happen in the first place become unnecessary.

Mitigations Rendered Obsolete

1. **Phishing Filters and Training Programs**:
   Phishing is one of the most common attack vectors, and entire industries have been built around mitigating its impact. Phishing filters attempt to catch fraudulent emails, and training programs teach employees how to recognize phishing attempts. However, with digital IDs and direct user interaction, phishing becomes irrelevant. Unauthorized users can no longer gain access simply by tricking someone into revealing their credentials because access is not granted based on transmitted data alone.

2. **IP Whitelisting**: Traditionally, IP whitelisting has been used to restrict network access to a predefined set of IP addresses. However, this approach can be circumvented by attackers using virtual private networks (VPNs) or proxy servers. With digital IDs and direct user interaction, network access is tied to the physical presence of an authorized digital ID, making IP whitelisting redundant.

3. **Multi-layered Authentication**: As discussed in previous chapters, systems use multi-layered authentication as a way to compensate for the weaknesses of single-factor authentication. But when true MFA is implemented using digital IDs, these multi-layered approaches become unnecessary. The digital ID itself provides multiple distinct factors (something you have and something you are), eliminating the need for additional layers.

4. **Intrusion Detection Systems (IDS)**: IDS are designed to detect suspicious activity on a network and alert administrators to potential threats. While these systems can still play a role in monitoring network activity, their necessity is greatly reduced when unauthorized access is prevented at the outset through digital IDs and direct user interaction.

5. **Encryption of Transmitted Data**: Encryption is a critical component of cybersecurity, used to protect data as it travels across networks. However, when direct user interaction is employed, the need to encrypt every piece of transmitted data

diminishes. The digital ID and its direct connection to the network ensure that only authorized users can access and transmit data, reducing the attack surface for encrypted data to be intercepted.

6. **Password Managers and Complex Password Policies**: Passwords have long been a weak point in security. Complex password policies and password managers are used to mitigate the risks associated with poor password practices. However, digital IDs eliminate the need for passwords altogether by relying on the physical possession of the ID and the user's biometric verification.

7. **VPNs (Virtual Private Networks)**: VPNs have been used to secure remote connections to corporate networks. However, they are often cumbersome and can be exploited if credentials are compromised. With digital IDs, secure connections are established directly through the ID, bypassing the need for a VPN.

8. **Anti-malware and Antivirus Programs**: While still important for endpoint security, the reliance on these programs decreases when direct user interaction is implemented. Malware and viruses often rely on exploiting weaknesses in user behavior, such as downloading malicious software. With digital IDs, unauthorized software downloads can be blocked before they ever reach the network.

9. **Two-Factor Authentication (2FA) via SMS or Email**: Many organizations rely on 2FA as an additional security measure. However, 2FA codes

sent via SMS or email can be intercepted or spoofed. Digital IDs make this type of 2FA unnecessary by providing true multifactor authentication that doesn't rely on transmitted data.

10. **Firewalls**: Firewalls are essential for protecting networks from unauthorized access. However, their role diminishes when digital IDs and direct user interaction ensure that only authorized users can access the network in the first place. Firewalls still play a role, but the burden on them is significantly reduced.

A Paradigm Shift in Cybersecurity

When digital IDs and direct user interaction are implemented, the effect on network security is not just a reduction in the need for certain mitigations but a complete paradigm shift. The cascading effect of securing the first point of contact (the network login) reverberates throughout the entire security architecture. Many of the traditional mitigation strategies that organizations have relied on become redundant because the vulnerabilities they were designed to address no longer exist.

The Shift from Mitigation to Prevention

The deployment of digital IDs and direct user interaction allows organizations to move beyond a reactive approach to cybersecurity. Instead of constantly patching holes and responding to threats as they arise, businesses can now take a proactive stance. By securing the first point of access, they eliminate many of the risks that have plagued them for years.

This shift from mitigation to prevention does not just simplify security; it also makes it more effective. When the primary attack vectors are eliminated, the need for complex, layered defenses diminishes. The result is a leaner, more streamlined security architecture that is easier to manage and far more difficult to breach.

A New Era in Cybersecurity

The introduction of digital IDs and direct user interaction fundamentally changes cybersecurity. By addressing the root causes of many security vulnerabilities, these two technologies render a host of traditional mitigation strategies obsolete. As organizations transition to this new approach, they can expect not only a reduction in complexity and cost but also a significant increase in security effectiveness. The future of cybersecurity lies not in the endless layering of mitigations but in the proactive prevention of threats at their source.

With an estimated reading time of approximately 6 minutes for 1,125 words, the estimated damage cost if compromised is $114 million.

CHAPTER 14

The Battle for Integrity in Cybersecurity

A Crossroads in Cybersecurity

The cybersecurity industry is at a crossroads. For years, the focus has been on developing solutions that patch vulnerabilities, mitigate threats, and respond to breaches. However, as we've explored in previous chapters, many of these solutions are reactive, addressing symptoms rather than the root cause of security failures. The introduction of digital IDs and direct user interaction represents a proactive approach to securing networks, but it also exposes a deeper issue within the cybersecurity industry: a lack of integrity.

Examining the Ethical Challenges in Cybersecurity

This chapter delves into the ethical challenges that have plagued cybersecurity, examining how the prioritization of revenue over genuine security solutions has led to a widespread failure to protect networks effectively. We will explore the importance of integrity in cybersecurity and challenge the industry to adopt a new approach that prioritizes real security over profit.

© Christopher Murphy 2025
C. Murphy, *Quantum Security*, Apress Pocket Guides,
https://doi.org/10.1007/979-8-8688-1240-8_14

Integrity As the Foundation of Security

Integrity is the foundation of any effective security strategy. Without it, all efforts to protect data, systems, and networks are compromised. Unfortunately, the cybersecurity industry has lost sight of this fundamental principle. The rush to market products, the pressure to meet quarterly earnings targets, and the allure of quick fixes have all contributed to an environment where the appearance of security is often prioritized over actual security.

The Misrepresentation of MFA Compliance

One of the most glaring examples of this is the universal misrepresentation of multifactor authentication (MFA). As we discussed in Chapter 10, the majority of products on the market today that claim to provide MFA, in reality, offer nothing more than single-factor authentication (SFA) disguised as MFA. This misrepresentation is not just a technical oversight; it is an ethical failure.

Consequences of Compromising Integrity

The consequences of this lack of integrity are far-reaching. Companies that believe they are secure because they have implemented so-called MFA solutions are left vulnerable to attacks that could have been prevented with genuine MFA. This false sense of security has led to countless breaches, resulting in trillions of dollars in losses, damage to reputations, and, in some cases, the collapse of entire businesses.

Impact of Profit-Driven Security Approaches

Moreover, the focus on revenue over security has stifled innovation in the industry. Instead of developing new solutions that address the root cause of security failures, many companies have opted to recycle old ideas, repackaging them as something new. This stagnation has prevented the adoption of truly innovative technologies, like digital IDs and direct user interaction, which have the potential to revolutionize network security.

A Call for a Cultural Shift in Cybersecurity

The cybersecurity industry must undergo a cultural shift. It's time for companies to prioritize integrity over profit and focus on providing real security solutions rather than temporary fixes. This means being honest with clients about the limitations of current technologies, investing in research and development to create better solutions, and being transparent about the effectiveness of the products and services they offer.

The Role of Cybersecurity Professionals

For cybersecurity professionals, this also means taking a stand against practices that prioritize revenue over security. It means refusing to sell products that don't deliver on their promises and advocating for solutions that genuinely protect networks. It means educating clients about the risks of relying on outdated, misrepresented, or inadequate security measures, helping them understand the benefits of adopting integrity-based technologies that offer true protection.

Digital IDs and Direct User Interaction As a Path Forward

Digital IDs and direct user interaction represent a path forward for the cybersecurity industry. These technologies address the root cause of most security vulnerabilities by ensuring that only authorized users can access secure networks. By eliminating the need for public logins, they remove a major attack vector and reduce the need for complex, layered defenses.

The Need for Honesty and Transparency

However, for these technologies to be adopted on a wide scale, the industry must first acknowledge the shortcomings of current approaches. This requires a commitment to integrity; being honest about what works and what doesn't, and making the necessary changes to protect networks effectively.

The Future of Cybersecurity Depends on Integrity

The future of cybersecurity depends on the decisions made today. If the industry continues down the path of prioritizing profit over security, we can expect more of the same: more breaches, more losses, and more damage to businesses and consumers alike. However, if the industry chooses to embrace integrity, to prioritize real security over ill-gotten revenue, and to adopt technologies that address the root cause of security failures, we can build a safer, more secure digital world.

The Battle for Integrity Is About Survival

The battle for integrity in cybersecurity is not just about ethics; it's about survival. As cyber threats continue to evolve and become more sophisticated, the need for real cybersecurity solutions has never been greater. The time to act is now.

A Clear Choice for the Future

The cybersecurity industry stands at a critical juncture. The choice is clear: continue with business as usual, prioritizing profit over security, or embrace a new approach that values integrity and focuses on real solutions. Digital IDs and direct user interaction offer a solid way forward, but only if the industry is willing to change.

With an estimated reading time of approximately 4 minutes for 878 words, the estimated damage cost if compromised is $76 million.

CHAPTER 15

Big Data vs. Network Security

The Value and Risks of Big Data

In the modern digital landscape, data is often referred to as the "new oil." It fuels decision-making, drives innovation, and offers unprecedented insights into consumer behavior, market trends, and operational efficiencies. However, the collection and use of big data come with significant security risks. As companies amass vast amounts of data, they become prime targets for cyberattacks. This chapter explores the delicate balance between big data and network security, focusing on how digital IDs and direct user interaction can enhance security without stifling the benefits of data-driven strategies.

What Is Big Data?

Big data refers to the large volumes of data generated by businesses and individuals every second of every day. This data is often unstructured, coming from a variety of sources such as social media, sensors, transactions, and user interactions. Companies harness this data to gain insights that can lead to improved products, services, and customer experiences.

© Christopher Murphy 2025
C. Murphy, *Quantum Security*, Apress Pocket Guides,
https://doi.org/10.1007/979-8-8688-1240-8_15

Challenges of Securing Big Data

However, as the volume of data grows, so does the challenge of securing it. Traditional security measures, designed for smaller, more controlled environments, struggle to keep up with the scale and complexity of big data environments. This has led to an increased reliance on mitigation strategies, which, as we've discussed, are often reactive rather than proactive.

The Security Paradox of Big Data

The very nature of big data presents challenges for network security. Data must be accessible to be useful, which often means it is stored in environments that are vulnerable to attack. Additionally, the sheer volume of data makes it difficult to monitor and secure effectively. This has led to a security paradox: the more data companies collect, the harder it becomes to protect that data.

Public-Facing Systems and Vulnerability

Furthermore, the collection of big data often relies on public-facing systems, such as websites and mobile apps, that interact with users over the Internet. These systems are inherently vulnerable to attacks, particularly when they rely on indirect user interaction, which, as we've explored, is susceptible to identity threats and other exploits.

Digital IDs and Direct User Interaction as a Solution

Digital IDs and direct user interaction offer a solution to the security challenges posed by big data. By shifting from public-facing systems to private, secure interactions, these technologies can protect sensitive data from unauthorized access while still allowing companies to harness the power of big data:

> **Securing Access at the Source:** One of the key benefits of digital IDs and direct user interaction is the ability to secure access at the source. Rather than relying on public logins or indirect methods of verifying identity, digital IDs ensure that only authorized users can access sensitive data. This reduces the risk of unauthorized access and makes it easier to control who has access to what data.

> **Reducing the Attack Surface:** By eliminating the need for public logins and indirect user interaction, digital IDs significantly reduce the attack surface. This means there are fewer opportunities for attackers to gain access to data, making it easier to protect big data environments from breaches.

> **Enhancing Data Privacy:** Data privacy is a growing concern for both consumers and regulators. Digital IDs and direct user interaction can help companies meet privacy requirements by ensuring that data is only accessible to those with a legitimate need to know. This not only enhances security but also builds trust with customers and stakeholders.

Balancing Data Access and Security: One of the challenges of big data is balancing the need for access with the need for security. Digital IDs and direct user interaction make it possible to strike this balance by allowing companies to control access without compromising security. By ensuring that only authorized users can access sensitive data, companies can protect their data while still leveraging it for insights and decision-making.

A Shift in Data Collection Practices

With the implementation of digital IDs and direct user interaction, there is a potential shift in how data is collected and used. In a traditional setup, data collection often involves tracking user behavior across public networks, websites, and applications. This type of data collection is inherently risky as it exposes both the data and the network to vulnerabilities.

The Controlled Environment of Digital IDs

By contrast, when a user interacts with a secure network through a digital ID, the interaction is private and secure from the outset. This means that data collection can occur in a more controlled environment, where the data is protected by the same security measures that protect the network itself. This shift not only enhances security but also reduces the need for extensive mitigation strategies.

The Future of Big Data and Network Security

As companies continue to rely on big data for strategic decision-making, the importance of securing that data will only grow. Digital IDs and direct user interaction represent a fundamental shift in how data can be protected, offering a way to secure big data without sacrificing the benefits it provides.

In the future, we can expect to see more companies adopting these technologies as they seek to balance the need for data access with the need for security. This shift will not only make big data safer but will also lead to more efficient and effective data collection practices.

Moving Toward Secure Big Data Practices

The conflict between big data and network security has been a major challenge for businesses in the digital age. However, the introduction of digital IDs and direct user interaction offers a path forward. By securing access at the source, reducing the attack surface, and enhancing data privacy, these technologies allow companies to continue benefiting from big data without compromising security.

With an estimated reading time of approximately 5 minutes for 944 words, the estimated damage cost if compromised is $95 million.

CHAPTER 16

The Future of Network Security

As we look to the future, the landscape of network security is poised for dramatic change. The introduction of digital IDs and direct user interaction has the potential to redefine how we protect our digital assets. This chapter explores the possibilities for innovation in network security and the challenges that must be addressed to realize the full potential of these technologies.

Ending Public Access to Secure Networks

One of the most significant changes on the horizon is the potential end of public access to secure networks. For decades, companies have relied on public-facing logins to manage access to their networks. This approach has been convenient but fraught with security risks, as it exposes the network to unauthorized access and exploitation.

Digital IDs and direct user interaction offer a different approach. By moving the login process to a private, secure environment, companies can eliminate one of the most significant attack vectors in network security. This shift would mark a fundamental change in how networks are protected, moving away from a reactive model of mitigation to a proactive model of prevention.

© Christopher Murphy 2025
C. Murphy, *Quantum Security*, Apress Pocket Guides,
https://doi.org/10.1007/979-8-8688-1240-8_16

Challenges in Scalability

One of the challenges facing the widespread adoption of digital IDs and direct user interaction is scalability. Large organizations with millions of users will need to implement these technologies in a way that is both efficient and effective. This will require new approaches to identity management, as well as the implementation of scalable solutions that can handle the demands of large, complex networks.

Despite these challenges, the benefits of digital IDs and direct user interaction make them worth pursuing. As companies increasingly recognize the limitations of traditional network security methods, the demand for scalable, effective solutions will only grow.

Blockchain Integration for Enhanced Security

Blockchain technology, known for its use in cryptocurrencies, also holds promise for the future of network security. The decentralized nature of blockchain makes it highly secure and resistant to tampering. When combined with digital IDs and direct user interaction, blockchain could provide an additional layer of security, ensuring that all interactions within a network are verified and recorded in an immutable ledger.

This integration could revolutionize how we think about network security, making it possible to create networks that are not only secure but also transparent and accountable. As blockchain technology continues to evolve, its potential applications in network security will likely expand, offering new ways to protect digital assets.

Anticipating Regulatory Changes

As network security evolves, so too will the regulatory landscape. Governments and regulatory bodies are already taking steps to address the shortcomings of current security practices, and the introduction of digital IDs and direct user interaction will likely accelerate these efforts. Companies will need to stay ahead of these changes, ensuring that they not only comply with existing regulations but also anticipate future requirements.

The move toward stricter regulations will drive the adoption of more secure network practices. Companies that embrace digital IDs and direct user interaction will be better positioned to meet these new standards and avoid the penalties associated with noncompliance.

Importance of Education and Training

As new technologies are introduced, education and training will be crucial to their successful implementation. IT professionals, network administrators, and even end users will need to be educated on the benefits and use of digital IDs and direct user interaction. This will require a concerted effort from both the private sector and educational institutions to ensure that the workforce is prepared to handle the demands of a more secure network environment.

Training will also play a key role in overcoming resistance to change. As with any new technology, there will be those who are hesitant to adopt it. Effective education and training programs can help ease this transition, demonstrating the benefits of digital IDs and direct user interaction and how they can enhance security without disrupting existing workflows.

The Road Ahead for Network Security

The future of network security is one of both challenges and opportunities. The introduction of digital IDs and direct user interaction represents a significant step forward, offering the potential to eliminate many of the vulnerabilities that have plagued networks for decades. However, realizing this potential will require a concerted effort from all stakeholders, including businesses, regulators, and educators.

As we look ahead, it is clear the network of tomorrow will be one that is more secure, more efficient, and more resilient. Digital IDs and direct user interaction will play a central role in this transformation, helping create a digital environment where security is not just a goal but a reality.

The future of network security is bright, but it will require bold action and innovative thinking to fully realize its full potential. Digital IDs and direct user interaction offer a path forward, but their success will depend on our willingness to embrace change and prioritize cybersecurity over convenience. As we move into this new era, the choices we make today will shape the networks of tomorrow. The time to act is now.

With an estimated reading time of approximately 4 minutes for 828 words, the estimated damage cost if compromised is $76 million.

CHAPTER 17

Implementing the Change

By focusing on ease of deployment, minimal disruption to existing infrastructure, and effective employee training, we'll outline how organizations can achieve a seamless transition to stronger, more resilient network security. These final steps will demonstrate how to unlock the full potential of this innovative cybersecurity model while safeguarding sensitive data from external threats.

Shifting to Digital ID and Direct User Interaction

Shifting from a traditional browser-based login system to a digital ID and direct user interaction model offers a seamless integration with existing infrastructure. Despite its profound impact on security, the implementation process is remarkably simple.

Step 1: Acquiring a New URL

The journey begins with the company acquiring a new URL, which will serve as the gateway to the client-side digital ID system. The significance of this step is that no changes are needed to the current network

© Christopher Murphy 2025
C. Murphy, *Quantum Security*, Apress Pocket Guides,
https://doi.org/10.1007/979-8-8688-1240-8_17

infrastructure. Once the digital ID technology is installed on the server side, this URL becomes the new secure entry point for authorized users.

Unlike a browser-based login page, which is publicly accessible and subject to numerous vulnerabilities, the new URL is private and accessible only through authorized digital IDs by the one-to-one relationship mentioned earlier. This ensures that sensitive login access is no longer exposed to the public Internet. The system operates alongside the existing infrastructure, allowing for a phased transition as employees are introduced to the new digital ID process.

Step 2: Associating Digital IDs with Employees

Next, the company's user table must be updated with a new field to store the public key for each employee's digital ID. This addition is the only technical modification needed to integrate digital ID technology into the company's infrastructure. Once an employee receives their unique digital ID, they can connect directly to the secure network through the private URL.

The digital ID itself serves as the employee's identification, eliminating the need for complex multifactor authentication (MFA) methods, which rely heavily on transmitted data and are susceptible to exploitation. The digital ID performs all necessary security checks, ensuring the user's identity is verified without the use of traditional browser-based MFA systems that are vulnerable to phishing, replay attacks, and other threats.

Step 3: Concurrent Operation

The transition period allows the digital ID system to operate concurrently with the existing browser-based login infrastructure. This is especially important for large organizations that may need time to fully distribute digital IDs to employees and train them in the new process.

During this phase, employees who have received their digital IDs will be instructed to use the digital ID system for accessing the secure network, while employees who have not yet transitioned can continue to use the traditional browser-based login. This flexibility enables a smooth, nondisruptive shift from the old system to the new one.

Step 4: Simplified Training

Training employees on the use of digital IDs is a simple and intuitive process. The core message is straightforward: when interacting with the company's secure network, use the digital ID. For all other browsing or public-facing activities, employees continue to use a browser.

This clear distinction between public and secure activity eliminates the confusion often associated with browser-based MFA. In the past, employees would be required to log into secure systems through the same browsers they used for general Internet browsing, creating opportunities for cyberattacks. By segregating public browsing from secure network interaction, digital ID technology closes a major security loophole.

Step 5: Final Step—Removing Public Login Access

The final and critical step in the deployment process is to remove the login page from the public website. After employees have been trained and the digital ID system is fully operational, the company can retire its public-facing login. This removes all public exposure to the login page, which is one of the most exploited entry points for cybercriminals.

By eliminating the need for public access to the secure network's login, the company dramatically reduces its attack surface. Phishing attacks, brute-force attacks, and other exploits targeting login pages are rendered irrelevant. Only employees with an issued digital ID can connect to the network, providing a new level of control and security that was previously unattainable.

Step 6: Realizing the Security Benefits

Once the digital ID system is fully deployed, the company benefits from a higher level of security that requires no ongoing mitigation. The digital ID technology inherently verifies identity, removes the risk of browser-based exploits, and eliminates the potential for successful phishing or replay attacks. Employees connect directly to the company's secure network using issued digital IDs, and sensitive information is protected from public exposure.

A Return to Simplicity and Compliance

The introduction of digital IDs and direct user interaction not only simplifies the process of accessing a secure network but also fundamentally transforms network security by eliminating public access vulnerabilities. Current MFA systems, which rely on data transmitted through browsers, have failed to meet regulatory standards for true multifactor authentication. Digital ID technology, by contrast, ensures compliance with the strictest regulatory definitions of MFA, using distinct, independent factors to verify identity.

Moreover, digital ID technology represents a return to simplicity with no complex infrastructure changes, no reliance on error-prone browser-based MFA, and no need for continued mitigation efforts. The digital ID system protects the network from the moment of interaction by verifying the presence and identity of the employee before allowing access to sensitive data.

As businesses adopt this model, the need for traditional cybersecurity products that provide layered protections or continuous monitoring will diminish because the network will already be protected at the point of entry, rendering many of today's common security measures obsolete.

The Broader Implications for Network Security

As we've explored, the transition to digital IDs and direct user interaction significantly enhances network security. However, this leads us to a broader conversation about the fundamental conflict at the heart of modern cybersecurity: public vs. private access. In the next chapter, we will address this inescapable divide and its implications, delving into why securing internal, private aspects of a company's network requires a different approach from the public-facing systems that currently dominate cybersecurity models. Understanding this conflict is essential for shaping the future of network security.

With an estimated reading time of approximately 5 minutes for 1,142 words, the estimated damage cost if compromised is $108 million.

CHAPTER 18

Digital ID As the New Endpoint

The modern concept of an endpoint in cybersecurity often centers around devices: smartphones, laptops, desktops, and even IoT devices. These devices are ever-present, always connected, and often vulnerable. When the device becomes the point of interaction with a secure network, it inherently exposes data and user credentials to the Internet. However, proving the identity of a device does nothing to prove the identity or presence of the user behind it. This distinction is where digital ID technology changes the game.

Rethinking the Endpoint

In the current network security model, devices are endpoints that exist whether the user is active or not. These devices are online when powered on, sometimes even when powered off, meaning they are always a potential target. Session data, soft tokens, cached information—all of it exists in this persistent online state, exposed and susceptible to interception or cloning.

Digital IDs fundamentally alter this paradigm by removing the endpoint from the device and placing it in the user's pocket in the form of an encrypted serialized identification. Unlike a smartphone or laptop, the digital ID is absent when it's not in use, leaving no trace on the local device or the broader network. This absence is not just theoretical; it is verifiable.

C. Murphy, *Quantum Security*, Apress Pocket Guides,
https://doi.org/10.1007/979-8-8688-1240-8_18

Presence vs. Absence in Network Security

When the digital ID is connected, it acts as a distinct physical factor tied to a specific user. When disconnected, the user ceases to exist on the network, eliminating impersonation risks. Without the digital ID, hackers cannot access session data or other user-specific credentials.

Consider this: proving a user's absence is often more valuable than proving their presence. In the case of breaches like the Oldsmar Water Plant or SolarWinds, had the network been able to verify that the specific employee's digital ID was not present, the system could have halted unauthorized actions, raised an alert, and shut down the session before any damage occurred.

Leveraging Verifiable Absence

In essence, *absence* becomes a powerful tool in defending against attacks. Instead of constantly worrying about whether a user's credentials have been stolen or misused, network security can rely on the physical absence of the digital ID to stop unauthorized access. This simple yet profound shift changes how we view user verification.

By shifting the endpoint from a device to the digital ID, network security takes a quantum leap forward. No longer are security measures tied to the vulnerabilities of devices that are always online. Instead, they are bound to an encrypted identification that is only present when connected. When the user disconnects, everything from session data to access credentials evaporates from the local device. Nothing is cached, and nothing remains for a hacker to exploit.

Transforming Trust with Verifiable Absence

This concept of verifiable absence not only protects against identity theft and impersonation but also introduces a much-needed layer of trust into the network security model. With digital IDs, organizations know with certainty that when a user is not on the network, their credentials cannot be misused. This moves cybersecurity from the realm of "mitigating risks" to actively preventing them.

In cybersecurity, we often focus on presence, on knowing when a user is connected and ensuring their actions are legitimate. But in truth, absence is just as critical. Further, when a system can truly prove presence, by default it can also prove absence. By verifying that an employee is not connected to the network, organizations can take preemptive steps to prevent attacks that rely on stolen credentials or identity theft.

Implementing Digital IDs As the New Endpoint

This change doesn't require a complete overhaul of network infrastructure. Instead, it involves issuing digital IDs to authorized users and integrating them into the current network security framework. The simplicity of the solution is what makes it so revolutionary.

Proving absence may seem like a subtle shift in thinking, but its impact is profound. With the deployment of digital IDs and the removal of device-based endpoints, network security enters a new era where identity theft, impersonation, and unauthorized access become challenges of the past.

With an estimated reading time of approximately 5 minutes for 893 words, the estimated damage cost if compromised is $84 million.

CHAPTER 19

The Inescapable Conflict: Public vs. Private in Cybersecurity

In modern cybersecurity, a fundamental flaw has persisted, compromising the very foundations of what it means to protect digital assets. This flaw lies in the inability of traditional cybersecurity practices to distinguish between public (not secure) and private (secure) activities. When these two fundamentally different types of interactions are commingled within a single security model, the result is a tangled mess of layered mitigations that fail to address the root cause of the problem.

Historical Context and the Evolution of Cybersecurity

To understand this flaw, we must first recognize the historical context in which the Internet and, by extension, cybersecurity developed. The Internet was initially designed for openness and accessibility, with security

© Christopher Murphy 2025
C. Murphy, *Quantum Security*, Apress Pocket Guides,
https://doi.org/10.1007/979-8-8688-1240-8_19

concerns taking a back seat. This was understandable in a time when the primary purpose of the Internet was to facilitate the free exchange of information, not to protect sensitive data.

As the Internet evolved, however, the need to secure private, sensitive activities grew. Yet, instead of creating a distinct model for these activities, they were simply layered on top of the existing, open framework. This led to a situation where the same network could host both a company's public-facing website and its secure login portal, with no clear separation between the two.

Challenges of Commingling Public and Private Activities

This commingling of public and private activities creates a significant challenge for cybersecurity. Public activities, by their very nature, are less secure because they are accessible to anyone. Private activities, on the other hand, require strict access controls and higher levels of protection. When these two types of activities are treated the same way, the security measures applied are inadequate for one or the other, usually at the expense of the private, secure activities.

The Reactive Approach and Layered Mitigations

In an attempt to address the vulnerabilities created by this flawed model, the cybersecurity industry has developed a plethora of mitigation strategies. Firewalls, intrusion detection systems, encryption, and multifactor authentication (MFA) are just a few of the tools used to try to protect networks from the growing array of threats. However, these strategies are often applied in layers, with each layer attempting to compensate for the weaknesses of the others.

The problem with this approach is that it is inherently reactive. Each new threat or vulnerability leads to the creation of another layer of security, but these layers do not address the underlying issue: the failure to separate public and private activities. Instead, they create additional layers of complexity and potential points of failure, making the system more difficult to manage and potentially less secure overall.

The Flaws of Layered Security

Layered mitigations, while necessary in some contexts, often serve as a Band-Aid over a wound that requires surgery. They address symptoms rather than the cause, leading to a situation where cybersecurity professionals are constantly playing catch-up, trying to defend against an ever-evolving landscape of threats without ever truly fixing the underlying problem.

Creating a Clear Separation Between Public and Private Activities

To truly secure a network, it is essential to recognize that public and private activities require fundamentally different approaches. Public activities, such as those that occur on a company's website, are meant to be accessible to the general public and therefore cannot be secured in the same way as private activities. Private activities, such as accessing internal systems or handling sensitive data, must be protected by stringent security measures that go beyond what is necessary for public-facing interactions.

The solution lies in creating a clear separation between these two types of activities. This separation begins with the network's architecture and extends to the methods used to authenticate and authorize users. For private, secure activities, this means moving away from the traditional, browser-based approach and adopting direct user interaction through digital IDs. By doing so, organizations can ensure that only authorized individuals have access to sensitive systems and that this access is not commingled with public, potentially insecure, access points.

A Philosophical Shift in Cybersecurity

The challenge of distinguishing between public and private activities is not merely a technical one; it is a philosophical one. It requires a shift in how we think about cybersecurity, from a reactive process of patching vulnerabilities to a proactive process of building security from the ground up.

Digital IDs and direct user interaction offer a path forward. By focusing on the unique needs of private, secure activities and recognizing that these needs cannot be met by the same methods used for public activities, organizations can create a more secure and resilient network. This approach eliminates the need for many of the layered mitigations that have become standard practice, allowing for a simpler, more effective security model.

Embracing the Distinction for a Secure Future

The inability to distinguish between public and private activities in cybersecurity has led to a model that is both overly complex and fundamentally flawed. By addressing this issue at its root, by separating public and private interactions and adopting direct user interaction for secure activities, organizations can move beyond the limitations of the current cybersecurity paradigm.

In the end, true network security is not about piling on more layers of protection; it is about making the right decisions from the start. By embracing the distinction between public and private and by implementing the technologies and strategies that respect this distinction, we can build a digital world that is not only more secure but also more aligned with the principles of integrity and transparency that are essential to trust in the digital age.

With an estimated reading time of approximately 7 minutes for 1,275 words, the estimated damage cost if compromised is $133 million.

CHAPTER 20

The Unified Quantum Security Model: A New Approach to Cybersecurity

As the digital landscape becomes increasingly complex, the limitations of traditional cybersecurity methods are becoming more apparent. Layered defenses, reactive security measures, and reliance on public-facing systems have proven inadequate in countering sophisticated cyberattacks. In response, a new paradigm is emerging that integrates advanced concepts like quantum theory into cybersecurity, creating a unified model that leverages digital IDs and the split interaction process to secure networks more effectively.

The Fragmented Nature of Traditional Cybersecurity

Traditional cybersecurity approaches often treat endpoint security, communication security, and network security as separate, isolated concerns. This fragmented approach creates gaps that can be exploited

© Christopher Murphy 2025
C. Murphy, *Quantum Security*, Apress Pocket Guides,
https://doi.org/10.1007/979-8-8688-1240-8_20

by cybercriminals. By addressing these components independently, organizations inadvertently leave their systems vulnerable to attacks that can bypass isolated defenses. The unified model seeks to eliminate these vulnerabilities by integrating all aspects of cybersecurity into a cohesive process that is controlled entirely by the network, not by third-party intermediaries or the user.

Key Components of the Unified Quantum Security Model

At the heart of this unified approach are three key components: direct user interaction, digital IDs, and the split interaction process. Together, these elements create a secure environment where every aspect of network interaction is controlled, monitored, and protected within a unified framework:

1. **Direct User Interaction**: Traditional methods often rely on indirect interactions, such as browser-based logins, which expose user credentials to the Internet and create opportunities for exploitation. The unified model replaces this with direct user interaction through a digital ID, ensuring that only authorized individuals can access the network, eliminating vulnerabilities associated with indirect methods.

2. **Digital IDs**: Digital IDs are uniquely serialized and encrypted tokens that serve as the user's identity within the network. Unlike passwords or other transmitted data, digital IDs are physical objects that must be present for the user to gain access.

This provides a distinct, verifiable factor in the
authentication process, making unauthorized
access nearly impossible.

3. **The Split Interaction Process**: The split interaction
   process is the defining feature of the unified model.
   By dividing the interaction between the user and
   the network into two distinct halves, one stored
   on the network and the other on the digital ID,
   full interaction only occurs when both halves are
   present and connected. This creates a secure,
   private tunnel for communication between the
   user and the network, isolating the interaction from
   potential threats on the Internet.

Advantages of the Unified Model

The unified model offers several significant advantages over traditional
cybersecurity approaches:

1. **Comprehensive Security**: By integrating all aspects
   of network interaction into a single process, the
   unified model provides comprehensive security
   that addresses vulnerabilities at every level. There
   are no isolated systems or independent processes
   for attackers to exploit; every interaction is secured
   within the unified framework.

2. **Proactive Prevention**: Unlike traditional models
   that rely on reactive mitigation strategies, the unified
   model is inherently preventive. By controlling
   access at the very first point of interaction and

ensuring that all subsequent actions are securely
managed, unauthorized access is prevented before
it can occur.

3. **Simplified Management**: The unified model reduces
   the complexity of managing multiple, independent
   security measures. With all aspects of security
   integrated into a single process, organizations can
   streamline their security operations, making it easier
   to monitor, manage, and maintain.

4. **Scalability and Flexibility**: The unified model
   is designed to be scalable, making it suitable for
   organizations of all sizes. Whether a company has
   hundreds or millions of users, the model can be
   implemented in a way that meets its specific needs.

Quantum Mechanics and the Split Interaction Theory

Drawing inspiration from quantum mechanics, particularly Niels Bohr's
split particle theory, the split interaction theory in cybersecurity involves
dividing the user–network interaction into two distinct parts. One half
of the interaction process is stored on the network, managing and
maintaining the public keys associated with the network's digital IDs. The
other half is stored on the physical digital ID held by the user, containing
the private key and other essential credentials.

This approach ensures that full interaction only occurs when
both halves are present and connected, creating a secure tunnel for
communication. This model effectively eliminates the need for public-
facing login pages and transmitted data, which can be intercepted or
spoofed, thereby significantly reducing the risk of unauthorized access.

The Future of the Unified Quantum Security Model

The unified quantum security model introduced by digital ID technology represents a revolutionary approach to network security. By splitting the interaction process into two distinct parts and controlling the entire process within the network, this model offers a level of security and control that is unparalleled in the industry. As organizations begin to adopt this model, they will not only protect their digital assets more effectively but also contribute to a more secure and resilient digital world.

With an estimated reading time of approximately 7 minutes for 1,255 words, the estimated damage cost if compromised is $131 million.

CHAPTER 21

The Urgency of Action

The journey through this book has laid bare the stark realities of our current cybersecurity landscape, revealing the vulnerabilities inherent in outdated systems and the false sense of security provided by conventional methods. We've traced the evolution of cybersecurity from its origins, highlighted the flaws in current practices, and introduced the transformative potential of digital IDs and direct user interaction. Now, as we reach the conclusion, one truth becomes inescapably clear: the time for action is now.

Moving Beyond Patchwork Solutions

For too long, the industry has relied on patchwork solutions, layering mitigation upon mitigation without addressing the root cause of security failures. The results are predictable, endless breaches, escalating costs, and a pervasive sense of insecurity. Yet, the solution is within our grasp. Digital ID technology, grounded in solid science and rigorous security protocols, offers a clear path forward. It's not just an enhancement; it's a fundamental shift in how we approach network security.

© Christopher Murphy 2025
C. Murphy, *Quantum Security*, Apress Pocket Guides,
https://doi.org/10.1007/979-8-8688-1240-8_21

The Simplicity of Implementation

One of the most compelling aspects of digital IDs and direct user interaction is the simplicity of implementation. The concurrent deployment model allows organizations to integrate this technology without disrupting their existing infrastructure. This means that the excuses often cited, cost, complexity, and downtime, are no longer valid. The minimal impact on current operations, combined with the immediate security benefits, makes the decision to act not just logical but imperative.

A Call for New Thinking in Cybersecurity

As Albert Einstein famously said, "We cannot solve our problems with the same thinking we used when we created them." The security issues we face today cannot be resolved by clinging to the flawed models of the past. True security can only be achieved when the foundation is built on solid science and unassailable security protocols. Digital IDs represent that foundation, shifting the endpoint from vulnerable devices to a secure, user-controlled identification system that leaves nothing to chance.

Prevention Over Mitigation

Benjamin Franklin wisely observed, "An ounce of prevention is worth a pound of cure." Digital ID technology is that ounce of prevention. By securing the first point of contact, the network login, this technology eliminates the need for endless layers of mitigation and reactive measures. It prevents unauthorized access before it can happen, providing a level of security that current methods simply cannot match.

The Imperative for Decisive Action

The challenges we face are not insurmountable, but they do require decisive action. Every day that passes without addressing the fundamental flaws in our cybersecurity practices is another day of exposure to risk, another opportunity for breach, and another step toward potential disaster. The concurrent deployment of digital IDs and direct user interaction removes any real excuse for delay. The technology is ready; the path is clear. All that is required is the will to act.

Building a Secure Digital Future

The time has come to move beyond the temporary fixes and half-measures that have defined cybersecurity for too long. By adopting digital ID technology and embracing a new model of network security, we can finally build a truly secure digital environment, one that is resilient, robust, and prepared to meet the challenges of tomorrow.

The process of securing our networks begins with a single step: choosing to lay a foundation built on solid science and proven security protocols. The future of cybersecurity is within our reach, and the opportunity to seize it is now. Let us not delay any longer. The path to a secure future is clear, and it starts with the decisions we make today. The time for action is not tomorrow, not next year, but now.

With an estimated reading time of approximately 5 minutes for 961 words, the estimated damage cost if compromised is $95 million.

Index

A

Authentication
    computer science, 13
    cybersecurity/network
        security, 17
    digital ID, 17, 18
    direct interaction, 14
    indirect
        interaction, 14
    MFA, 15, 16
    SFA, 15
    transmitted data, 17

B

Big data, 85
Big data *vs.* network security
    challenges, 86
    controlled
        environment, 88
    data collection, 88
    digital IDs, 89
    digital IDs and direct user
        interaction, 87, 88
    risk, 85
Blockchain technology, 92
Brute-force attacks, 23

C

Credential-based attacks, 65
Cybersecurity, 11, 12
    cyber threats emergency, 3
    digital IDs, 6, 7
    Internet and vulnerabilities, 1, 2
    MFA challenges, 5
    public face login/MFA, 4
    reactive approach, 3
Cybersecurity industry
    challenges, 79
    cultural shift, 81
    digital IDs and direct user
        interaction, 82
    integrity, 80, 82

D

Digital ID, *see* Digital identification
    (digital ID)
Digital identification (digital ID), 14
    cost, 70
    cost constraints, 28
    direct interaction/binary
        security, 28
    financial services/regulatory
        compliance, 67, 68

C. Murphy, *Quantum Security*, Apress Pocket Guides,
https://doi.org/10.1007/979-8-8688-1240-8

Printed in the United States
by Baker & Taylor Publisher Services